IN PRAISE OF THE MEANINGFUL RETIREMENT GUIDE

This is a book everybody should read, not only those with the tag "employee". In a world where jobs evaporate as morning dew, and in an underdeveloped country like Nigeria where one "bread winner" caters for seven to ten mouths, every person connected with the bread winner should watch what he or she does as a hawk watches its kitten.
Paul Uduk
CEO, Vision & Talent
Author, *Wealth Beyond Your Imagination* and *Bridges to the Customer's Heart*

Beautifully rendered! The Meaningful Retirement Guide dwarfs all previous publications I have read on retirement. It is a must read for all workers, administrators, retirees and management science researchers.
Cosmas Udofot, PhD
Retired Permanent Secretary
Akwa Ibom State Civil Service and former Director, Union Bank of Nigeria.

This is the best book every worker should read. It is a billionaire's collection of facts that gives street experience for successful retirement without much stress. The book provides ideas for next income opportunity and guides in healthy living. I equally recommend it to employers of labour to enhance employee resilience.
Nse Okponung
Entrepreneur and Founder, African Directory for Co-operative Societies.

This is a very thorough and masterly exposition of Retirement for what it truly is. The worker is instructively guided on how his retirement can be peaceful, profitable and pleasurable phase of another life, and a totally new experience to really look forward to.
Emmanuel Inyang
CEO, Quantum House Publishers

THE MEANINGFUL RETIREMENT GUIDE

A Time-tested Path to Financial and Social Relevance for Every Worker.

PAUL UDOFOT

authorHOUSE®

AuthorHouse™
1663 Liberty Drive
Bloomington, IN 47403
www.authorhouse.com
Phone: 833-262-8899

Published by AuthorHouse 03/08/2021

ISBN: 978-1-6655-1886-4 (sc)
ISBN: 978-1-6655-1885-7 (e)

Library of Congress Control Number: 2021904627

Print information available on the last page.

Foreword

The Meaningful Retirement Guide is coming at a time when the world challenges are forcing many into early retirement.

The author has employed the evidences of history and the testimonies of living personalities to show that retirement should not be an end to human life activities and achievements. He has shown cases of many who had made great contributions during their retirements.

The book contains information on options that are available to retirees that can make their lives meaningful. The business options that a retiree can consider, with guides on how to develop a Business Plan, is well presented. The possibility of Consultancy engagements and Agricultural enterprises that are open to retirees are also examined.

Common challenges that confront retirees such as Stress, Health Matters, Finance and Social Pressures are fully discussed with possible guides that can make the retirees to successfully manage them.

The inclusion of personal life stories of some retirees will surely help many to look forward to their retirement with optimism. I commend this book to all who want to fulfill their destinies and make new adventures in retirement. Indeed, the retirement years can be converted to years of fulfillment and greater glories.

Olusola Oyewole, PhD
(Professor of Food Microbiology and Biotechnology)
Former Vice-Chancellor, Federal University of Agriculture, Abeokuta, Nigeria, and Former President, Association of African Universities, Accra, Ghana

Foreword

Acknowledgments

I am greatly indebted to individuals and institutions whose sources of information were used in the course of writing this book. Paul Uduk provided the initial motivation for the writing through his *Book Writing Clinic*, Aniekan Mbah and Enoh Nelson showed an uncommon interest towards its completion. Afahaide was helpful in the cover design and the editors were excellent in their job which they did cheerfully. I am eternally grateful.

For my late father,

Sir Malachy O. Udofot, *KSJ*, who opened my eyes to the treasure in retirement, I love you and owe so much to you.

10% of Author royalty from the sales of this book will be donated to my *Alma Mata*, Holy Family College, Abak, through the Old Boys Association.

'As to methods there may be a million and then some, but principles are few. The man who grasps principles can successfully select his own methods. The man who tries methods, ignoring principles, is sure to have trouble'. Raph Waldo Emerson

CONTENTS

INTRODUCTION

A man who does not plan ahead will find trouble at his door. Confucius

The stories as captured in the following scenarios are true.

Scenario 1: George, 53 years and Mary, 50, husband and wife respectively, were doing well as mortgage professionals in the United States until the financial crisis of the 2009. In the early days of the crisis, they felt secured from the turbulence of the crisis. Months later, they lost their jobs and were forced into retirement. They started depending on their savings for survival. Within a short period, their home plummeted by over fifty percent and their egg nest shrunk considerably. An advice from a Consultant further shrunk their fortunes. Unable to maintain their lifestyle in retirement and sensing a chaotic future life, they relocated to Las Terrenas in Dominican Republic, a global retirement destination.

Scenario 2: Saviour Maxwell was 26 years old in 1985 when he started work as an administrative officer in the government service. He had a brilliant career and never missed a promotion except once when he could not be evaluated because of an accident that kept him hospitalised for almost two years. In the year 2003, he lost his wife through a strange disease that defied all medical attention. He was saddled with the responsibility of becoming a single parent and raising three children. In 2010, he remarried and the new union is blessed with a child. Saviour's wife works with a bank. In 2019, Saviour left the service in retirement in line with extant rules of the Service. He had expected a seamless transition into retirement. The gratuity which Saviour had expected to use in starting a new life in retirement has not been paid even after one year. The wife has been very generous and supportive. In the course of events, the wife was relieved of her bank appointment in a mass retrenchment exercise occasioned by the unstable global economy. Saviour feels betrayed by the entire system and blames his current situation on consequences of retirement.

Scenario 3: In the Japanese island of Shikoku, a retiree, Hayato Koki was saved an embarrassment by his son who showed up when he missed the pension payment in one of the designated months in the last quarter of 2018. The Japanese government pays its retirees six times a year on the 15th of even-numbered months. For a minor mistake of his, Koki could not make the payment schedule for the period. With no other source of income in retirement except the payment, life would have been unbearable for Koki during the period if the son had not intervened. Another retirement issue!

Scenario 4: For Patricia Michael, life has never been dull. Patricia has always been lucky both in school and at work. As an oil industry worker, she had the privilege of many foreign trips, and she lived well with her family. At retirement, the children were all grown up and working except for the baby of the house who was about finishing her Master's degree programme in Civil Engineering. Pat was handsomely paid her severance benefits when she retired. But, she was duped of the entire amount by a group of fraudsters, who may have been trailing her for about a year before her work disengagement. The proposal they had presented to her looked genuine and seemed to have matched her dream life in retirement. She was so badly affected that, but for her investments in landed property, she would have been reduced to a beggarly level. She however had consolation in her children and husband who stood by her. Few years later, she got very sick and money was urgently needed to fly her overseas for a special medical attention in Israel. She could not make the trip as she died before one of the properties could be sold. In his funeral tribute to his wife, Pat's husband attributed her death to retirement-related matters.

Samuel Emmanuel Chikodi (not real name) who had retired as a School Principal and having completed all retirement documentations, said thus in frustration: 'I voluntarily retired from the Imo state civil service to pursue other interests about 12 years ago. After waiting endlessly for my pension and other accrued benefits to no avail, I decided to go back to my first love, Civil Engineering. But for that stroke of luck, only God knows how I would have been able to survive with my family'.

On November 3, 2020, *The Punch* newspaper carried a headline '*Soldiers disperse protesting pensioners in Calabar*'. They were apparently protesting nonpayment of their entitlements. And perhaps in a seeming twist of events, retired soldiers were on the receiving end some few months later. The *Channels Television* reported on Wednesday January 15, 2021 of large numbers of retired soldiers visiting the Federal Ministry of Finance headquarters in Nigeria to protest non-payment of benefits.

The above persons had worked, made careers and retired. They had enjoyed their career life and had expected the bliss to continue in retirement. But, this never happened. I am sure you would not want to share in their varied experiences. They all had frustrating retirement experiences which are common to many people across the globe. In many cases, retirement does not turn out as many would want. Frustration, anxiety, loneliness and sadness have become familiar features. When you fail in retirement, you would end up defeated, disappointed and perhaps a failure! Many people end up facing this obvious situation. This is because you may not have the opportunity to right certain wrongs of your career life.

Retirement comes when nerves would have been weak, bones thin, job gone, influence waned and health challenges come knocking! Funding retirement planning process has remained one of the biggest economic and social challenges of the 21st century. Generally, retirees who are the target of such planning process end up despondent, traumatised and some even die untimely. They are bored, discriminated against and the poverty severity index is highest within the retiree age bracket. In many cases, retirees simply exist. They need help, counsel and support. This book which is based on results of researches, personal stories and observations across the globe is intended to provide needed counsel and support. It is to guide the reader into a meaningful retirement life of promise and purpose.

You may currently be working. Work is good!

Work plays an important role in the development of the adult personality, and makes a significant contribution to the quality of life we live. One is easily described related to the work he or she is involved with; the teacher, doctor, pilot, engineer, dock worker, civil servant and soldier among others. The extent of work is expressed in the fact that a large proportion of a nation's income is paid to workers as salaries and wages. The significance of work is further expressed in newspaper and television headlines as they report work-related matters like Gross Domestic Product (GDP), tax issues, employment, strikes, capacity utilization, downsizing, school placement and in recent times, artificial intelligence.

But, there comes a time the motivation or capacity to work dwindles either voluntarily or in a forced circumstance, no matter the level of one's mental alertness. There, comes retirement! The transition from work to retirement can be difficult and retirees may take years to acclimatise to their new status. And retirement on its own has become an unending ubiquity.

Reading this book to the end will change a worker's disposition to retirement. The experiences, insights and retirement circumstances will assist the retirement planning process. Martha Washington, wife of a renowned American former President once said 'I am still determined to be cheerful and happy, in whatever situation I may be; for I have also learned from experience that the greater part of our happiness and misery depends upon our dispositions, and not upon our circumstances'. This is true even in retirement!

In planning towards retirement, it may not just be about finance, though it is very important. You may be stockpiling assets and resources which may not serve your expectations but, an aim at meaningful retirement which emphasizes relevance, peace of mind, family interest, self-esteem, good health and a sense of purpose should rather attract your attention and interest. Retirement bliss is possible; it is your personal responsibility to actualise it.

So, what is your disposition towards retirement? If you are interested in an amazing retirement life, then say this simple prayer and read further:

Lord, I thank you for my years of labour. Help me convert the best of my experience, talents and skills into a meaningful retirement life, Amen.

CHAPTER ONE

UNDERSTANDING RETIREMENT

Retirement is a blank sheet of paper. It is a chance to redesign your life into something new and different. Patrick Foley

History of Retirement

Retirement is generally associated with age-related exit from paid employment which comes with compensation. This can be as a result of job loss, health challenge, difficult boss and co-workers, financial incentive, as well as social or family responsibilities. Jimmy Carter, a former United States President, describes it as liberation from mandatory duties. It can be described as an undisputed phase of life if one examines the words of Confucius (circa 500 B.C.):

> *At fifteen I set my heart upon learning. At thirty, I planted my feet firm upon the ground. At forty, I no longer suffer from perplexities. At fifty, I knew what were the biddings of Heaven. At sixty, I heard them with docile ear. At seventy, I could follow the dictates of my own heart; for what I desired no longer overstepped the boundaries of right.*

My interpretation of the above passage is that there are certain expectations or realities at different phases of our life. Regarding work, fifteen to thirty years period may be the struggling or apprentice phase in career which stabilises at forty. Fifty confirms a plateau that slopes downwards from sixty years. The southwards slide may represent the beginning of retirement years in modern day normal work calendar.

For the adult, retirement is the third phase after school and work life phases. It is believed to have been introduced into modern governance in Germany in the 1880s during the reign of Chancellor Otto Van Bismarck in an attempt to scuttle the rising popularity of Communism in Europe. It was a period when the Communist ideology was literally setting the world, especially Europe on fire due to the intellectual writings of Karl Marx and Frederick Angels. For a stable reign, he successfully persuaded the parliament to outlaw paid employment at a particular age bracket which most of his perceived Communist enemies belonged. Pronto! Other industrialised countries curiously copied this into their Labour relationships and it has since become the tradition in paid employment to leave work at a certain period of one's work tenure.

Retirement is both an event and process. It is an event because there is an exact work exit date or period, and a process because it continues thereafter till death. This seemingly harmless act of leaving work is known to exert a great impact on key social issues such as healthcare, employment, immigration, increasing family separation and poverty, among others. The rising numbers of retired persons in many countries and the associated consequences have generated growing interest and excitement in the retirement planning process. To the workers, the idea of having to stay without work and its privileges and at the same time being socially relevant becomes a concern. Equally, the challenge of replacing the retiring personnel as well as paying their entitlements is what occupies the attention of the employers. Managing this process to achieve a balance has always been bedevilled by inherent challenges and in some cases with controversial outcomes. It has remained an unresolved case in many countries across the globe.

In Nigeria for instance, there has been an increasing public sector debt in pension settlements. The State and Federal governments are said to owe their former employees to the tune of trillions of Naira. Whenever retirement payments are made, they are not adjusted to reflect current inflationary realities. In Japan, there has been an increasing crime rate of people above 65 years in the past twenty years. For instance, shoplifting is reported to have become rife within the retiree age bracket. The global Corona virus pandemic had successfully eased the retirement-related strikes in Russia and France in 2020.

In the United States, Social Security calculations indicate guarantee retirement payments until 2037[1]. Thereafter, payment can only cover 78% of benefits, according to *Social Security Bulletin.* In Kenya, there was a reported case of legal entanglement over the non-remittance of over 2.7 billion Shillings (about 25.3 million USD) deducted from salaries of the State broadcasting agency workers, but not channelled to the retirement benefit scheme. There is a litany of such cases across the globe. In UK, State Pension recognises different ages for men and women and the numbers have been changing since 1948. There is hardly any country in the world without unresolved retirement-related issues thus impeding broad-based meaningful retirement endeavours.

Who is a Retiree?

I will leave my reader to answer this question but, with a guide. A *2013 Merrill Lynch and Age Wave* study on retirement attempted an answer to this question. The study indicated that 31% of respondents believed that the retiree is one with financial independence, 23% said the fellow that stop work permanently, and 18% were of the view that it is the person that left a principal work or career. 15% of the respondents indicated anybody receiving social security benefits while 7% and 6% of the respondents picked on the person of a certain age and one being eligible for an employer pension respectively. In the United States of America, the retirement age is 65 years. The Nigerian Civil Service retires its staff at 60 or anyone who has worked for 35 years. A University Professor and Supreme Court Judge retire at 70 years. Generally, the conventional retirement age varies from country to country ranging between 50 to 70 years. In this book, the retiree will be described as anyone of 50years and above, whether working or not. 50 years is the minimum number for early retirement globally and the number is prescribed in Cambodia and Thailand.

Effects of retirement

It has been observed that there is a general lack of sufficient knowledge regarding retirement hence the apparent trepidation on the part of the retiree and in some cases, sharp practices associated with it, especially in developing countries where inadequate record keeping remains a major challenge - age may be falsified, fraud committed and records altered in the hope to influence the retirement flow. Certain realities may have informed the general opinion people have about meaningful retirement. These can be summarised as follows:

i. Income and influence will reduce. Apart from income which drastically reduces upon retirement, the work place confers an identity, power and impetus on the worker. Olusegun Obasanjo, Nigeria's former two-time Head of

Government once said regarding the influence a person's job confers on one thus: 'the soldier has no power without the uniform'. He was actually emphasizing the reason behind his government's decision to retire serving military officers who were exposed to politics. To him, their continued stay could easily trigger a coup, hence their disengagement. Retiring them from the military stripped them of identity and demystified their influence.

ii. There have been an increasing number of persons known to you who have reached the retirement age in different fields of endeavour with apparent societal irrelevance. Dr. Phyllis Moen aptly captures 'we plan our careers but, we don't plan our retirement'.

iii. Life expectancy is higher than what retirement systems are designed for. With wonders in modern medicine and nutrition, people now live longer than any other time in modern human history.

iv. You are no longer popular in the former office you held. Another *king is anointed* to take your place and the fellow may never appreciate anything you did.

v. Usurpers of your family land and traditional titles are afraid of your presence and feel you will demand for what is rightfully yours. Usurpers are always there, common and very many. They vary from close to distant relatives and also those who are not related to you, but are powerful enough to take whatever belongs to you. It is to be noted that these people are very dangerous and do not relinquish things easily.

vi. There are other challenges like perceived wrongs done in the past. At your perceived weak moment, they want to address it since they could not address it then because of your privileged position and the powerful instruments at your disposal.

vii. You are not connected with the society. You are returning to a 'new' environment having stayed away for long because of career assignment.

viii. Retirement may present an opportunity for former colleagues to get back at you. Your relationship with trusted assistants may become testy. Reference will be made of those that enjoyed your confidence, ran your errand and curried your favour.

ix. Your spouse and family members may rebuff you as the '*shine*' is no longer there. Spousal relationship may suffer terribly just as there is an opportunity for it to grow from strength to strength. Spending more time at home may open your eyes to some dirty habits you may not have noticed. Too much of your presence may even irritate your spouse and family members.

x. Only few persons including family members you assisted will return. The late Dr. Olusegun Agagu narrated his story as former deputy governor of Ondo State in Nigeria. While in office, there was a dedicated room for Christmas gifts but on leaving office in November 1993, only 22 Christmas cards were received the following month, according to him.

xi. Some of your past career activities/events will make you sad. Adams Oshiomhole, an activist-turned elected governor of Edo State of Nigeria has openly expressed his regrets in the choice of his *Khalifah*. Their disagreement snowballed into a major political crisis that extended beyond the boundaries of the State. You may not have been a governor but certain decisions and indecisions you made will certainly anger you.

xii. You are no more employable as employers would prefer the younger and a more teachable generation.

xiii. You may have retired for wrong reasons. A new technology, office politics or a false accusation may have caused your retirement. This is likely to cause bitterness and its attendant consequences.

xiv. Your well-accumulated money can never buy time or happier times. Perhaps the story of Markus Persson who went into retirement at 36 as told by *Mirror Newspaper, Sept. 2, 2015* may suffice. When Persson, a 36 years- old Swede apps developer got $2.5 billion from Microsoft for creating and selling his video game company, *Minecraft*, everything looked set for him 'to retire, rest, eat better and have more fun'. How wrong he was! With all the fancies and fantasies procured, there was still a vacuum in him to be filled. The newspaper reported that the bored billionaire later wrote on a social media platform, Twitter thus: 'the problem with getting everything is you run out of reasons to keep trying, and human interaction becomes impossible due to imbalance'. Later on, he added '...hanging out in Ibiza with a bunch of friends and partying with famous people, able to do whatever I want, and I've never felt more isolated'. He also complained of losing a girlfriend he had fallen in love with to someone else as the girl was scared off by his wealth.

xv. Your investment may not yield the expected returns. Investment climate remains one of the most unstable occurrences in the world. The instability can be initiated by financial, trade, oil-market driven or a sudden health pandemic like the novel Corona virus disease of 2019.

xvi. There is always a gap between what is needed and what is served. Financial experts have developed formulas for calculating adequate savings which should last through retirement but, how many persons have successfully hit the target? Even when you can, what of your health and family relationship?

xvii. You may be lonesome. This may not only be in the physical absence of people, but a psychological problem that may eventually lead to depression and other health disorders. Missing the perks and privileges of office may not completely detach you from your office.

xviii. Your entitlements may not be paid or they may be delayed as documented in the 2019 studies of Huixin Bi and Sarah Zubairy. Nigeria is a clear example where 'workers are abandoned immediately they leave office'. There are instances where retirees block major roads in protest of non-payment of their entitlements that span many years.

xix. You had no retirement plan. Ordinarily, retirement plans should commence on the date of first appointment but, most people procrastinate till the twilight of their exit.

xx. Your children may still be in school, jobless or wayward.

xxi. You may have issues with the place of habitation. Your present house may be too big for you as a retiree or in a location not suitable with your present status.

xxii. Your community may reject and antagonise you as it remembers your non-contribution towards its development at the time you were working or simply to get at you.

Ask President Trump about the New York and Florida communities!

xxiii. You may be scammed by fraudsters or even misled by professionals. Your estate can be sold without your knowledge. Some may come as do-gooders reminding you of family and ancestral rights in other people's possession, all in the process to dissipate your energy.

xxiv. You may lose your spouse. This will certainly have a debilitating effect on your person and personality. There is also the retired husband syndrome where the wife suddenly starts resenting the husband. A study has shown a higher level of divorce among those of retirement age bracket.

xxv. You may develop age-related sicknesses. Ageing is part of life process and it comes with ailments, some of which are expensive to manage.

The Class of Workers and Peculiarities

Work may influence one's ability in achieving a meaningful retirement. As a worker, you are either self-employed, a Civil Servant, serving in a military or para-military establishment or as a corporate official. The self-employed works for himself/herself and earns income from the business, skills or profession rather than receive a specified salary from an employer. He chooses when and how to perform the business and enjoys all the profits as appropriate. This may be done in partnership with others or as a sole proprietor.

The civil servant may work for government or international service organisation. He works under relatively loose rules when compared to other classes of workers. There is more time for social activities outside work and he does not work under pressure. The work schedule requires group result with a slow bureaucratic structure and fixed procedures. They generally seem to do well in retirement as the work description seems to fit into the retirement rhythm.

The military or para-military personnel work in a regimented organisation with command structure and strict rules. They are involved in rigorous training in hostile conditions even in peace times. They have expanded ego of self importance and believe in *esprit de corps*. The military operates a non-contributory, government funded retirement system.

The corporate work is profit-orientated, with timelines, busy schedules, long hours, targeted results and monetary reward. Corporate workers may not have a fixed procedure of work but there are internal control mechanisms to check abuses. Mistakes are not accepted except when it is minimal. There is complete severance on exit.

Behavioural Pattern of Workers towards Retirement

The vast majority of workers already know that they should plan for retirement. People know they will certainly stop working at a point but their mindset will influence their behaviour on retirement planning. The behaviour is generally patterned based on social news, attitude, faith and general experience. Psychologists believe behaviour is influenced by willpower, knowledge and skill, social motivation and ability, structural motivation and structural ability.

Willpower is believed to be the genuine desire for desired change just as exposure to adequate knowledge and the acquisition of skills has the capacity to influence along the line of the acquired resources. Social motivation relates to behaviour based on association with friends, colleagues and family members. The influence of mentors and support groups is described as social ability while structural motivation is about giving oneself a treat at every success point. And, structural ability is the understanding given to the anticipated consequences of behaviour.

In the work place, commonly identified retirement-related behaviours are:

(i) The *Mayana Syndrome* – Those who exhibit this behavioural pattern procrastinate on every aspect of retirement plans until they are officially notified of their retirement date. There are cases where some workers become oblivious of their retirement date and therefore failed to plan until officially reminded by the employer. Such workers usually respond violently to such reminders and obviously would not have a fulfilled retirement life.

(ii) The *Assumers* believe some other persons will take care of their retirement life responsibilities. Their expectation may be on children or family members. How wrong! The Holy book admonishes 'trust no one'.

(iii) The *Passive Players* are just bored about retirement plans. To such people, 'God has predestined everyone and everything' hence 'what would be, will be'.

(iv) The *Spenders* make good salary, live well and with few debts but have nothing set aside for retirement. These are people that 'fizzle out of existence' upon retirement.

(v) The *Blamers* blame everyone - the employers, government, salary structure, economy and even family members except themselves for retirement woes. A case was mentioned of a senior officer who blamed the system for his 'sudden' retirement, few days to his mandatory disengagement.

(vi) The *Talkers* are so well informed about every retirement issue but lack evidence to collaborate the knowledge. They may even work in pension offices.

(vii) The *Victims* are workers that had failed sometimes and the failure mentality has refused to leave them. They may have failed in marriage or organisational power play and they allow themselves to be discouraged by such earlier failures.

(viii) The *Cliff Hangers* have just enough to make ends meet but never enough for the next day, not to mention retirement.

Are You Ready to Retire?

Before answering this question, I want to remind the reader that all events in life are mirrors of your thoughts. Great thinkers have always admonished that the greatest limitations are self-imposed, and the greatest obstacle to success is mental obstacle. I therefore strongly advise that you overcome built-in prejudices towards retirement. Ask questions for clarifications and liberation of thoughts. Pertinent questions have the capacity to enlighten and guide.

For a meaningful retirement life, answering the following questions and similar ones in affirmation helps evaluate your readiness to achieve the success:

(i) Do you believe you are more than your present work?

(ii) Can you recreate your life in retirement?

(iii) Have you drawn out a list of five major things you had always wanted to do?

(iv) Do you have a retirement budget?

(v) Have you reached the retirement age?

(vi) Have you informed your spouse about the intending retirement?

(vii) Can you reconnect with people that had given you joy in the past?
(viii) Do you see yourself continuously taking family responsibility?
(ix) Do you have a strong desire to contribute positively to your community?

A fulfilled retirement life may not be the ultimate as it may leave you with a vacuum of always comparing yourself with others. Though it is normal and even healthy to compare who you are and how you are doing against how others are doing, it is better to spend some thoughts on your own measures. Those are the only points of lasting importance in your life.

I want to end this chapter with a piece of advice with this anonymous quote: '*you should retire from obligations of paid work and its stress on your terms with your health intact before it is too late, on the day of your choice, on a sizeable investment, with your family's interest in mind, under the impression you have made the right choice into something of interest and satisfaction*'. Meaningful retirement is beyond self; it must be expected, planned and it abhors idle and sedentary lifestyle.

CHAPTER TWO

PROVEN ESSENTIALS IN RETIREMENT

Funny things about retirement, it kills more people than work ever did. Malcolm Forbes

Major Concerns for Retiree

Evidence-based studies including various *Merrill Lynch and Age Wave*[2] as well as *Hartford Fund Retirement*[3] Reports have shown some fundamentals which are critical to meaningful retirement. Though the studies were conducted in the United States, the results would not be significantly different if generalised to other environments. Understanding the identified indicators and giving due attention to them will expose you to the right knowledge needed to set and implement retirement goals. They will help you examine various scenarios and potential outcomes for possible trade-offs as well as provide the means to mitigate inherent retirement risks. That retirement is expensive, costing almost three times the average cost of a home, underlies why it must be taken seriously.

One major point in retirement is its changing role. The former idea of retiring to rest is fast becoming history. Today, retirement is seen as a period of reinvention and self-recreation. It is considered to be time to explore options and to put into practice long-held ideas or time to actualise dreams which were held down by routine work engagement.

It is thought of to be a time to write memoirs, connect more with the family, and translate hobbies into business, and volunteer knowledge and know-how towards impacting on the society. Retirees now seek greater purpose, stimulation and social engagement; and fulfilment. The result is in the launch of new businesses outside earlier work experience and exposure. Now, seven out of ten persons would want to work in retirement as against the earlier notion of declining work engagement in retirement.

Increasing life expectancy beyond the 20 years retirement plan, is not financially sustainable without employment. My mother, may God rest her soul, lived 27 years post retirement. She had kept herself busy with gardening and dedicated certain hours of the week for prayers for the Church. She had earlier worked for 35 years and had obtained a university degree. Ordinarily, staying idle would have been difficult for her. She was very strong until her death in 2015 from an incurable heart disease.

Equally, over the years, financial reliance has shifted from employers to employees affirming the changing role of work in retirement. But, motivation for post-retirement work is known to go beyond the need for money. In the 2014 *Aegon Retirement Readiness Survey*, 50% of respondents said they continued working because they had enjoyed their career, 45% said they wanted to keep their brain alert, 24% indicated government benefits were less than expected, 18% claimed it was the general anxieties about retirement income needs, and 14% indicated that retirement income was less than expected. Another 14% said the employer retirement/pension benefits were less than expected, while 11% of respondents claimed unplanned financial obligations. 10% of the studied group said they had not saved enough on a consistent basis and 5% were known to have taken a career break. Another 5% were unable to find full-time work and 16% of them gave other reasons.

For those working, there are the *Driven Achievers*, who tend to be workaholics and enjoy work in retirement. They constitute about 25% of the total number of retirees, 54% of the people in this category are known to have felt financially prepared for retirement. They are known to have their own businesses.

Thirty-three percent of retirees belong to the *Caring Contributors* category. Those in this group seek to give back something worthwhile to their community and may work on a non profit basis. Males make up 47% of persons in this group. Workgroup friendship and social connections would always attract the *Life Balancers* back to work. Though they need the extra money from work, they seek the kind of work which has fun and is less stressful. They had taken steps to prepare for retirement.

The *Earnest Earners* of about 28% of the entire number always need money to pay their bills; those in this category would have regrets and resentments about working at this time of their life.

The changing nature of work in retirement is worthy of note. Should you work? Do so on your terms where your interest, working hours, stress level, expected salary, skills and indeed clearly defined goals, are taken care of.

Health remains a major issue as 81% of retirees indicate health-related concerns. Maintaining a healthy status remains a major challenge especially in economies without defined elderly healthcare schemes. Health remains an important retirement priority alongside that of one's spouse. As one enters the retiree age bracket, certain ailments become noticeable. Managing these sicknesses can be a challenging liability

The place of residence is very important in retirement. The previous house may have been work-determined and no more suitable in retirement. In Nigeria, cases abound of big mansions which are either poorly maintained or completely abandoned due to dwindling fortunes arising from retirement. Children of such owners would have left in search of livelihoods leaving the parents with meagre resources which cannot keep such big houses in proper shape. House type, location, and its affordability remains a source of retirement fulfilment. It is not advisable to live in a rented apartment or continue paying mortgage in retirement

Family cohesion assists and assures peace of mind. How well and united family members are, is a point of concern to the retiree. The school fees, extending a hand of assistance to those family members in need, children's marital bliss or their career success have a great influence on meaningful retirement.

The retiree at the point of leaving paid employment is usually anxious, confused and full of apprehension. At this point, he is vulnerable to scammers and fraudsters as well as a having a health challenge. Counselling from professionals will be most useful.

I will not fail to mention the issue of finance. Money plays a major role in retirement and human relationships. Salaries, houses, cars, health issues and even retirement entitlements and many other transactions are calculated in monetary values. Towards achieving a blissful retirement, setting a financial goal is useful. Experts have suggested the need for savings. They have even gone further to determine the needed amount to take one through retirement based on certain criteria including pre-retirement income, returns on investments and other expected inflows.

Financial establishments are busy encouraging people to save. The question remains: who benefits from their 'savings' campaign? Their low interest rates may only make one a millionaire on paper, but poor in the real sense of it. It may not be wrong to say that it is irresponsibility to trust someone else with your future.

The truth is that it is actually very difficult to determine the exact amount of money one needs to sustain life in retirement. Taking Nigeria for example, such calculation say, in 1988, would produce a failed result say about 20 years later due to the general economic environment and activities in the international market. In specific terms, the financial crises of 2008 – 2009 exposed the risk of aggressive investment strategies; and the frequent adjustment of petroleum prices with its attendant inflation rates would have greatly rendered the figure inaccurate. The continuous downward movement in the capital market for five years running and the hammering of the economy as a result of the novel Corona virus pandemic further changed the narrative. And, Nigeria has little or no influence in the global economic arena.

As important as money is, experts would advise against "accumulating as much wealth as possible" but rather admonish on "saving enough to have financial peace of mind" The sage's advice has always been on contentment.

Grappling with Savings for the Future

One of the biggest challenges of individuals and organisations is how to decide to save for the future. The discipline to save for the future is so perverse despite acclaimed advantages. But, one must strive to save despite the challenges. For retirement, surveys have indicated that individuals are not saving sufficiently. Specifically, one of such reports stated thus:

> According to a recent Survey by the Employee benefit Research Institute, four out of ten American workers state that they are not putting any money aside for retirement
>
> A recent report in New Zealand concludes that many individuals are either "unwilling or not able" to save enough for retirement, adding that at 30percent of households spend more than they earn.

> A survey from the Bank of Ireland reveals concern that even those who are saving are not saving enough, adding that only about 52 percent of workers aged 20 to 69 are investing in a pension at all.
> Aside from government, employers themselves are increasingly concerned about their employees' level of saving. A recent survey by Hewitt Associates finds that only 18 percent of large employers in the United States are confident their employees are saving enough for retirement - OECD

It takes a lot of discipline to save and worse still for a long term purpose. This is further compounded by slave payments as salary, hard economic and social realities and outright suspicion of the system especially in developing economies. Perhaps, it is worthy of note to state that saving money does not make one rich. Rather, it is the direct product of what one does with the money one has! To assist in ameliorating some retirement challenges, the Federal Government of Nigeria initiated the Contributory Pension Scheme (CPS) in 2004. All workers have the opportunity to participate in the scheme. This scheme appears to be more sustainable. Before then, government retirement liabilities were made from yearly budgetary allocations with associated shortfalls and outright non payments in many cases.

The CPS focuses on individual responsibilities and employee co-operation as retirement benefits are compulsory and contributory. Employers and their workers jointly contribute towards retirement benefits which are dispensed upon retirement. According to the amended Act, eighteen percent of an individual's annual salary (made up of eight percent from employee and ten percent from the employer) is invested in a personalised and portable account by a Pension Fund Administrator (PFA) for subsequent use as gratuity and monthly pension allowance upon the retirement of the said individual.

Upon retirement, 25-50% of the lump sum is paid as gratuity with the calculation based on age, gender, last salary and net asset value in the retirement account. The balance is paid on equal monthly allocation for a minimum quantifiable period of 18 years and 22 years for males and females respectively. Thereafter, if the person is still alive, the interest that may have accrued over time is used. Discussion with retirees indicated the money is not always sufficient for their needs. Personal investments should complement the official scheme.

The CPS is however laced with operational challenges and unending agonies for the would-be beneficiaries. Of the 36 States of the Nigerian federation, only four States and the Federal Capital have attained a high level of compliance with the CPS including funding the accrued rights of their workers. Despite this, there are issues with payments to would-be benefiting retirees. As at 2020, retired workers in these four States and Abuja who had retired as far back as 2018 were still not paid their entitlements. Retired federal government workers who participated in the scheme were not faring better.

Generally, the operations of the CPS are not well understood by most people just like that of its most common American counterpart, 401k, which derived its name from a section of the country's Internal Revenue Code. It is therefore the responsibility of the worker to ask questions on grey areas of its operation. Individual and specific questions which can clarify identified issues are suggested since there is 'no perfect size which suits everyone'. Pension Consultants can be encouraged to assist in this regard.

But, can I save enough for my Retirement?

Even though there is no consensus among experts on how to calculate the exact pre-retirement savings target, there is need to know the process that can give an understanding of this significant issue. Just like we check our blood pressure for information, the information on retirement savings and general personal finance in retirement is important in setting a post-retirement support goal.

Even though many formulae have been developed to determine how much one should save towards retirement, I will not bore you with complex mathematical calculations. The simplest ones to answer the above question may suffice.

One of such is the 4% rule of thumb principle which guides on withdrawals from retirement savings. The idea came about as a result of a study conducted by Trinity University professors. The study started in 1926 and ended in 1976, a period of 50 years. The result of the study was published in 1998 and updated in 2011. The principle is based on the study of historical data of stock and bond in the years of the study which also witnessed great global events including the first and second world wars, The great depression, Korean, Cold and Vietnam wars, the 1990s technology Bubble and the Spanish Flu which killed over 100million people. The principle indicates that 4% is the maximum percentage people could withdraw from their retirement portfolio in the first year of retirement, so that the money does not get exhausted up to 30 years period, even after adjusting to accommodate inflation. Though popular in the United States, it does not hold up in other developed countries. Even so, how do I calculate mine? Assuming your retirement saving is N15,000,000.00, then a yearly withdrawal of N600,000.00 (which is 4% of the total amount) would sustain you for up to 30 years in retirement.

The *multiply by 25* rule calculates how much you will need to save for retirement. This approach is based on your current expenditure multiplied by 25. For instance, if your current expenditure is N600,000.00 per annum, then you should save N15 million for retirement.

Equally, based on a survey of consumer finances in the US in 2016, *Merrill Lynch* experts have suggested the following retirement savings rates based on current pay and in line with age categories. For those of ages 18-29, it is 0.7 times of their current salary that has to be saved and, for the people of between 30-39 years, 1.3 times of their current pay that have to be saved for retirement purposes. People of 40-49 age bracket need to save 2.8 times of their current salary towards retirement while those in the range of 50-59 years have to meet 4.9 times savings target of their current salary for the same purpose. For the people of 60-64 age category, they have to save 7.4 times of their current salary towards meeting their retirement savings target according to the experts' report.

But, how many people can successfully save to meet these targets? Please, do not be intimidated! Personal lifestyle, family size, health status, life expectancy and economic environment are some of the factors that influence the use of money in retirement. As I have indicated earlier, meaningful retirement is beyond money. No matter the amount accumulated, it can go in one fell swoop. Therefore, I will not suggest a specific 'silver bullet' but will rather counsel on a 'lead bullet' of consistent ways of improving financial education over a long period of time. I also believe that goodwill can even nurture a nest egg.

Though money is essential, it is the expenditure pattern that matters the most. For instance, a *2015 Employee Benefit Research Institute* report on old persons' likely expenses on key areas like housing, food health, clothing transportation, entertainment and others showed a pattern. For all ages ranging from 50-85, housing expenses peaked at 46.25% with food at 13%, transport was 11%, health at 10.5%, entertainment was 9%, others stood at 6.75% and clothing trailing at 3.5%. So, an individual may have no housing issues but very challenging health issues. The expenditure pattern can guide the pre-retirement financial planning process. Creating inner sense of abundance and meaning in retirement begins with the ability to manage what one has and not necessarily the amount saved. Certainly, it is generally agreed that, if one is disciplined enough to save, say 20% of his income, such a fellow can easily live on 80% of the present income in retirement without adjusting expenses.

Please see more on the CPS in the Appendix.

CHAPTER THREE

GENERALS IN RETIREMENT

> *For the best verse hasn't been rhymed yet, the best house hasn't been planned, the highest peak hasn't been climbed yet, the mightiest rivers aren't spanned; Don't worry and fret, faint hearted, the chances have just begun, for the Best jobs haven't been started, the Best work hasn't been done.* Berton Braley

Despite apparent difficulties, some people have made great accomplishments in retirement. Though some of these may appear weird and funny, they would inspire and encourage succeeding generations in their plan towards meaningful retirement. Some of them include the following:

1. Noah Webster – An American textbook pioneer, political writer and prolific author was a lawyer by training who owned a private school for writing. The famous *Webster's Dictionary* compiled and named after him, was published when he was 68 years old.
2. At 105 years, Edith Kirkmeyer is said to be the oldest Facebook user in the world. In her words, 'when I was 95 years old, my children bought me a computer, a printer and digital camera, and turned me loose'. She participates in voluntary service

every day. She says "I have been volunteering at Direct Relief for 40 years, a humanitarian organisation that sends medical aid around the world. Even if it's just addressing the envelopes or writing 'Thank you' notes, it's very meaningful for those of us that do it. It really feeds my soul....We can win our adversities with love".

3. Clara Barton at 59 years old founded the American Red Cross with her experience as a nurse during the American Civil and the Prussian wars. She achieved widespread recognition delivering lectures on her experience in wars. She died in 1912 and was inducted into the National Women's hall of fame in 1973.
4. Dr Pius Okigbo who died at the age of 74, saw the need to update his skills and went for computer training at the age of 70 years. A renowned Nigerian Economist, he obtained his MA and PhD from North Western University in the USA.
5. Benjamin Franklin was an American polymath. His picture is embossed on the 2009 United States dollar bill. He was noted for his thirteen virtues of temperance, cleanliness, order, humility, silence, resoluteness, frugality, industry, justice, moderation, chastity, tranquillity and sincerity. He is the only founding father whose signature appears on all the documents founding the United States. At 80 years old, his prayers were known to have calmed nerves in the American constitution drafting assembly. He died at 84 years.
6. Flo Meiller, a 79 old great-grandmother had created a new world record in pole vault competition for her age category when she scaled about 6.7ft height in 2010.
7. Theodore Mommsen, in 1902, became the oldest person to receive the Nobel Prize in Lliterature at the age of 85 years. His works had significant impact on the German civil code.

8. 100 years old Dr. Walter Watson, the oldest practising physician in the United States, was still seeing few patients in 2020. He is known to have delivered between 15,000-18,000 babies, fondly referred to as 'Watson babies'.
9. Mary Baker Eddy at 54 founded the Christian Science Monitor. The book was selected as one of the '75 books by women whose words have changed the world'.
10. Larry King (born Lawrence Harvey Zeiger) celebrated 50 years in broadcasting at 73.
11. In 1998, an American Democratic Senator, John Herschel Glen, Jr. became the oldest man on earth to fly into space. He was aged 77 at the time.
12. In 2016, history was made in the Nigerian legal profession when an 80 year old Enebeli Pius Chuka, was called to the Nigerian bar following his success in the Bar final examination conducted under the supervision of the Council of Legal Education.
13. Sir Andrew Iheakaran at 86 was inducted a member of the Chartered Institute of Taxation of Nigeria, 26 years after retirement as Director of Imo State Board of Internal Revenue.
14. Muhammadu Buhari at 72 years became an elected president of the Federal Republic of Nigeria after three futile attempts in 2013, 2007 and 2011. He had earlier retired from the Military having been overthrown as Military Head of State in a palace coup in 1985.
15. The world's oldest head of government is Muhahir Mohammad of Malaysia. He became prime minister at 92 years. I met him in Kuala Lumpur in 2012 as a retiree prime minister having earlier served as prime minister between 1981 and 2003. He looked quite physically strong and was mentally alert.

16. Kentucky Fried Chicken, arguably the world's most favourite fast food restaurant was started by Col. Sanders, who got his breakthrough at 62 years of age. He sold his business in 1964 for $2 million and became a salaried brand Ambassador. He died in 1980 at the age of 90.
17. The story of Nigerian modern banking may not be complete without the 'grandmaster' of banking, Chief Michael O. Balogun. After a failed attempt at heading the then ICON Merchant Bank, he retired to set up his company in 1977. The company subsequently floated the First City Merchant Bank in 1982 which later transformed into First City Monument Bank. The bank is doing well in the Nigerian business environment.
18. Dr Asikpo Essien-Ibok, who calls me his son (non-biological) was a university don cum activist. He took to farming after retirement. He owns one of the biggest and well-organised farms in Akwa Ibom State of Nigeria. The farm employs many and provides opportunity for university students' practical agricultural engagement. He is very involved, very active, and mentally alert and frequently drives himself to the farm at 75.
19. Joao Havelange who died at the age of 100 in 2016 can never go unmentioned in the history of modern football. He became FIFA President at 56 and occupied the seat for over 24 years.
20. I will not fail to mention Dr. Enefiok Ene Essien. He motivates me in several ways. A former university lecturer at the University of Lagos, he later left for industry practice with the Ibru Organisation, a multi-sector business outfit in Nigeria. In retirement, the children were all grown-up, some had become State commissioners, lawyers, pharmacists,

computers experts, medical consultants, among others. He would simply have 'rested' and 'rusted', but not so for him. He returned to his familiar turf as a university don in his 60s to share his experience in business and research ending with a book entitled *Entrepreneurship: Concept and Practice.*

21. Tony O. Elumelu has attracted attention more as a retiree than when he was at the driving seat as the Managing Director at United Bank for Africa. His African-funded philanthropic Foundation is committed to investing $5,000 each in 1,000 young entrepreneurs per year across 54 African countries. He was voted as one of the *Time100 Most Influential People* in the world in the year 2020. Assisting the younger generation with start-up funds, I am sure, may give him greater joy and fulfilment than his previous assignment as a bank chief.
22. Olpha Selepe, a retired Primary School teacher became a pop sensation at 65. With a stage name of *GeeSixFive*, her music topped South Africa's *iTunes* chart. She had earlier registered for a PhD programme after a successful Master's degree, all after retirement.

All these people achieved these feats in retirement or at the age they would have easily 'rested to enjoy the fruits of their labour' and had their mental capacity frozen. But, they had persisted, persevered, set personal retirement goals and above all, believed in themselves. The experience they had, talents they honed, the character and values they cultivated and the vision they created for themselves aided in their achievements in retirement. Clearly, no matter the circumstance in which one leaves a job or has reached the proverbial retirement age, there is space for undeniable achievement, excellence or fulfilment.

I am sure the 80 years old traditional ruler in Western Nigeria, Alafin of Oyo, Oba Lamidi Olayiwola Adeyemi III would have made history when he welcomed three sets of twins within a year in 2018. He may not have retired from child-bearing endeavours but, having children may not necessarily occupy the mind of most people in his age bracket. And getting three sets of twins within a year for someone of his age can never go unnoticed. Identifying and following through activities of inner joy will certainly add up to a meaningful life in retirement.

CHAPTER FOUR

TIME MANAGEMENT IN RETIREMENT

Most of us spend too much time on what is urgent, and not enough time on what is important. - Steven Covey

Have you ever given a thought of a typical day in retirement? I clearly understood the impact of this question during the novel Corona virus disease lockdown period. Just before then, I was handsomely rewarded for a job I had done. During the period, my salary alongside those of my colleagues was stopped because of labour – related disagreement with the Federal Government. As a result of the salary stoppage, the Trade Union called on our members to down tools until all issues were settled.

The above circumstance presented to me in a typical "retiree" situation. I could no longer visit the office, the consultancy fee earlier paid would now become my gratuity and there was no school fees stress as everyone was indoors owing to the lockdown. I could pay my domestic staff and money was not much of a problem. With so much time at my disposal, one would think, I would have prayed more, exercised more, cleared my table, read books I had always wanted to, and perhaps write books or apply for research grants. Most of these expectations never materialised hence the inclusion of this chapter title.

I had fallen into the general complaint phrase of 'if I had more time', but here was I with all the time. And, how could I be given more time when, everyone has the same number of hours, days, weeks and years as long as they live! The equal allocation of time to everyone makes it a very important and unique resource. It cannot be stored, extended, reversed or even fast-tracked. The poor, rich, worker, and retirees all have the same allocation. It is so important that almost everything is built around it: time of birth, employment, duration of events and retirement, among others.

Carefully utilised, the advantages of managing time are many. You will have greater control over your time, work smarter, be less stressful and organized in your endeavours. Your professional reputation will not suffer, deadlines will be averted and a work-life balance will be achieved. The difference between success and failure can easily be summarised in the use of time as people say, it waits for no man. Technology, opportunity and development are all products of time.

Someone once said that the 'African time syndrome' which is the non-adherence to scheduled time, is the reason for African developmental-related challenges. Ninety-two percent of people are known to fail on their long term goals due to time management related challenges like procrastination, laziness and inability to prioritize effectively. Time, when optimally organised assures interpersonal relations, job satisfaction, reduced anxiety and guarantees good health. It actually releases 'more' time and exposes one to other opportunities. This is because things are done, planned and executed at the appropriate time and known schedules. This describes the Pareto or 80/20 principle where the minority of efforts leads to a majority of results. Explained further, 80% of major achievements come from 20% of allotted time properly used. Therefore, determine and address the activities which fall into the 20% portfolio first, and deal with the rest 80% later. This may sound contrary to what most people normally expect. It is not in the quantum but the value attached into the usage. Indeed, studies have proved true the principle. For instance, a 2016 survey conducted by *www.vouchercloud.com* indicated that an average UK office worker only accomplishes three hours of work each day no matter the length of physical presence in the office.

The importance and value attributed to time especially in the past few decades have created an industry in time management. There are books written, researches conducted and conferences held in time-related subjects. Peter Drucker, the all-time respected Management expert, believes time should be managed as a resource just like people manage money, human and other resources. Someone once said 'each time I have time-related issues with anyone on our first day of meeting; it often turns out that the relationship wouldn't easily blossom'.

People with conscious effort of managing themselves are often successful in their endeavours. My late mother in her retirement years would sleep at about 10pm to be awake at about 5am the following day. She would spend about 30minuites for meditation and thereafter her bathe before coming out of her room. At about 7am, she would go downstairs where she would spend substantial part of the day before moving upstairs again at about 5pm. The garden within her compound and domestic chores occupied her day. This routine adopted since the death of my father in 2003, was her practice and it worked well for her.

How can Time be managed?

Something which is open to everyone at equal quantity cannot be managed. Time management is self management. By so doing you control your schedule and efficiently take charge of every second of the day. It is applying yourself to utilising time to achieve long term goals. So, the right question should be: how do I manage myself to achieve my set goals based on the 24/7 allocated every other person?

i. The first step is to acknowledge you are a time waster. If your yesterday was well spent, your tomorrow would have been different. This acknowledgement should lead to a change in attitude and encourage self discipline and clearer focus on the future. Therefore, audit your time and remove unnecessary distractions. This must be done in line with your expected goals. The essence is to fish out the 'culprits', which magnify the waste as well as justify the 'congratulatory' addition for the goody-goodies. The culprits may include visitors, social media engagement, popular activities, telephone calls, television watching and pleasant activities. The goody-goodies are planning, value-created activities, prioritising and focusing on key targets and goals on daily future time bases.
ii. Organise time for every task and attempt to follow through. Prioritise tasks, break projects into small steps and set a time limit for each task. Get a daily routine which you can adjust if daily goals are not met. Use to-do-list which should not be too long. A long list will lead to anxiety in the morning and a possible frustration in the evening. Emphasis should be placed on the most important tasks of the day. Doing so may not bring a perfect outcome but would have successfully identified and destroyed the major 'stealer' of time, procrastination.
iii. Divide your activities into four, namely: (a) Important and urgent which should be completed right away. Examples are

pressing projects and deadlines (b) Important and not urgent tasks should be given more and strategic attention as they help in long term goal attainment. They include relationship building, planning and recognising opportunities (c) Urgent and not important activities like some phone calls and meetings may be delegated or minimised and (d) Not urgent and not important activities like pleasant and popular activities like mindless web surfing and too much Television watching should be eliminated as much as possible.

iv. Attempt one thing at a time. 'This one thing will I do', *Philippians 3:13.* Continue with a task until done. For instance, are you reading? Then forget the phone! Leaving tasks that have been started half-completed will further delay the course, and cause distractions. To Henry James, 'nothing is as fatiguing as hanging on an uncompleted task'. Plan your day ahead. In the words of Mignon McLaughlin 'for the happiest life, days should be rigorously planned, nights left open to chance'. It is generally believed that the most creative part of the day is the morning period. Spend your mornings on the most important tasks. Consider waking up early and cutting your Television watching time, rather focus on result-oriented activities.

v. The phrase 'better done than perfect' should be the underlying principle in your time management process. Spend less time in little improvement in an area considered not good enough but, rather spend the time on another item or activity. You can never be perfect in any task as there is always room for 'improvement'. And, it is not advisable to jump from one activity to another. You should allow enough time to clear your thoughts before getting involved in another task.

vi. Organise your work space and keep a file on every subject even as you batch similar activities. Doing so will save you the time searching for missing items. A *Pixie Lost and Found Survey* indicated that Americans spend a total of 2.5 days in a year searching for misplaced items.

vii. Learn to say 'no' to certain events, activities and persons. Saying so allows for self assessment for an adjustment. 'No' is a beautiful and powerful word that sets boundaries. Always saying 'yes' can constitute a time management challenge. Be real and always focus on your personal daily goal.

viii. Time management practice acknowledges the fact that you will work with people. Relationship should not be transactional but built on long term basis, which naturally adds value. Team members should avoid working on deadline driving projects as such have the tendency to cause projects failure, stress and burnout leading to crisis management. Do not over commit yourself; delegate or outsource tasks as much as it is possible. Doing so will free you and leave room for energy re-calibration.

ix. Embrace technology as much as it is possible.

I will end this chapter with the words of a Greek shipping magnet, Aristotle Onassis: 'I have learned the value and importance of time: therefore, I have to work two additional hours per day and in that way, I gain the equivalent of one additional month, each year'. Do you desire a life of meaning in retirement? Then, manage your time properly.

Figure 1: Sample of Time Management Assisted -To-Do Form

	Monday	Tuesday	Wednesday	Thursday	Friday	Saturday	Sunday
05:00AM							
06:00AM							
07:00AM							
08:00AM							
09:00AM							
10:00AM							
11:00AM							
12:00PM							
01:00PM							
02:00PM							
03:00PM							
04:00PM							
05:00PM							
06:00PM							
07:00PM							
08:00PM							
09:00PM							

CHAPTER FIVE

THE BUSINESS OPTION

I realised that according to the life expectancy tables, I had 25 years to go. What was I going to do with 25 more years? I was in a little town with 600 persons and no job – Jimmy Carter

A former American President, Jimmy Carter, 54 at the time, made the above quotation when he lost his presidential re-election bid in 1980. When I checked last in 2020, he was still alive. About him, the British Broadcasting Corporation, BBC once commented:

He's often held up as the best example of what to do after your time as US president comes to an end. Jimmy Carter, whose foreign policy problems tainted his presidency, has since worked for humanitarian causes, as well as working in international diplomacy and writing several books. In 2002 he was awarded the Nobel Peace Prize and at the age of 92 he is still involved in charitable projects such as building homes for disadvantaged people.

Even if he had all the money and good health in this world at retirement from the White House, he would have died of idleness, boredom and depression without engaging himself. Yakubu Gowon, a war time Nigerian military General and head of government, left for the University of Warwick in the United Kingdom at his overthrow. Forty-one years old at the time, he had ruled for nine years. He studied to the PhD level and was 85 in 2020. There is need for the business option, an engagement, a preoccupation, an activity and therefore I urge you act fast.

Business engages, tasks the mind, creates an expectation and may also frustrate in failure. It creates energy, changes pattern and adds value to the society. Business creates employment as the demand for jobs consistently exceed the supply and modern careers are found within individuals than in organisations.

Understanding Business

Business is an activity which seeks profit by providing needed goods and services to others. Hence, an activity that seeks to intentionally defraud may not be categorised as business. The activities must solve people's problems and the expected profit may not necessarily be monetary even though money is needed to oil its operations. For instance, non-profit organisations like the Red Cross, the Church, the Mosque, NGOs and similar organisations need money for the administration of their missions.

For a meaningful retirement, the business option provides an opportunity for self recreation, mental stimulation and everyday engagement. The experience, talents and knowledge from earlier work can enable a fulfilment. This may also come in several ways including chronicling your work experience. Reno Omokri, a former spokesman to President Jonathan of Nigeria, for instance was a number one bestselling author in 2017 when he published his memoir.

Perhaps the idea of setting up one's company may be a motivation for the business option. It could be such a business which would satisfy your longing for a work culture, authentic and sustainable attributes capable of bringing out the best in workers. Certainly, this will satisfy an inner desire. Continuing in what one loves doing can be satisfying. The counselling opportunity, the advocacy, the teaching engagement, the marketing ideas and negotiating skills among others, may still require some form of expression or transfer. It makes one articulate and in touch with current realities. Ray Ekpu, a founding editor of *Newswatch Magazine* for example, continues to express his good prose-writing skills in other newspapers, after leaving the *Newswatch* several years ago. His fans look forward for his articles which I am sure he derives enjoys supplying them.

A retiree can be part of solving the unemployment problems of a country. Any business that is created will require the services of workers that will make careers and livelihoods. Setting up a business therefore presents an opportunity to freely choose like-minds to work with. Helping others grow has been proven to enhance health, a vital ingredient of life.

Seventy percent of workers are known to be enduring their work. They just work for survival without any satisfaction. What a relief if a retiree creates his /her own environment of work without a dress code, rules, restrictions and bureaucracy. Life expectations from business can create one's definition of success outside those pronounced by bosses.

Business Ideas

Ideas are many but, as always advised; one must choose something of passion. The option one settles for should be something you love, something one is at ease with, something one can be proud of. For instance, I cannot own a pub because of my nature. A pub owner must always be around, very sociable and be the last to leave. I may not have the capacity to express such traits. It is worthy of note that any business one does not supervise closely may not succeed as one may be easily fleeced by the workers. This may not be applicable to large scale businesses where the services of professionals for different functions can easily be procured. Small businesses need nurturing like the attention given a young child.

Business ideas include bakery, water packaging, book writing, catering services, school ownership, monogramming, waste management, furniture manufacturing/marketing, transport, soap making, writing business plans, food processing, retailing, events management, refrigerator assembling, tailoring services, pet plastic bottle manufacturing, fruit drinks/ice cream production, tissue paper manufacturing, computer services, phone sales/repairs, grocery shop business, hospitality and philanthropic services.

Retiree Business Experience

Following a passion[5]

Nearly 20 years ago, Bonnie Zwack retired from a successful career in real estate in Minneapolis and moved with her husband, Neil, to Southern California. While playing golf, she met new friends who were grieving the loss of a parent and looking for ways to relocate the surviving parent. In response, Zwack researched ways to assist those who wanted to move a loved one to the area and provide care for them. In 2010, at age 70, she opened Always Best Care of Desert Cities, which provides senior services. "I was completely unfamiliar with the home health industry, but my innate desire to help others is what motivated me to immerse myself into the business," says Zwack, who now lives in Palm Desert, California. "Once your passion is identified, the hard work will feel effortless and the rest will fall into place."

Creating something new[5]

After working as a costume designer in the motion picture and TV industry for 35 years, Kerry Mellin of Simi Valley, California, struggled with arthritis. She dealt with the condition in various ways, including taping her hand to the broom when sweeping to reduce thumb pain. Thinking there had to be a better way to deal with grip issues, she teamed up with other family members to develop a grip aid. "We made 1,000 prototypes," Mellin says. "We obtained two patents, trademarks and started our business." Today Mellin is the designer and cofounder of EazyHold, which is now used at more than 4,000 hospitals. "While baby boomers do use our product, 90 percent of our product is sold to infants and children with severe disabilities," Mellin says. "To invent something that was so needed, yet so technically simple, is incredibly rewarding. Every day parents post pictures of their children using our product, telling us how excited they are that their child is able to eat by themselves, or drink by themselves, or write or paint by themselves."

Turning Ideas into Business

It is often said that a business starts with an idea - whether a bank, a manufacturing outfit, a marketing organization, it all starts with one person's idea. If the initial ideas were discarded, the breakthroughs we have today would not happen. But, the ability to turn ideas into feasible creative entities lies in the knowledge of business management techniques as well as the ability to manage through problems when they arise. Timing is also very important as an idea may come either too early or too late. I will give an example: Sometime in the early 1980s, someone in Nigeria proposed and actually set up a private university. The idea was not well received by the military authorities that ruled at the time. They could not imagine individuals setting up universities. The proponents of the idea escaped prosecution by sheer luck! Thereafter, statutes were made to outlaw private universities. But today, there are several private universities in Nigeria.

Equally, ideas are easily discarded when you allow yourself to be persuaded by all shades of opinion: 'is it possible?', 'I had tried that before', 'put it into writing', 'how is that your problem', 'why not go with tested ideas? These and similar other comments may hinder and derail your business path towards a meaningful retirement.

What Kind of Business?

I always have difficulties answering the above question whenever asked during my seminars sessions. Perhaps on individual basis, one normally attempts a suggestion. What is important is to first of all understand the business value chain, which are all the activities within a particular business that are needed to deliver its products or services. The activities include economic, financial, socio-political, technological, legal and ecological issues. It is normally advisable to build a business within and not outside the value chain. The value chain of the tomato puree manufacturing business, for an example, may start with the planting of tomatoes through its processing and ends with the final user through marketing. Questions like: 'should I go into the planting, processing or marketing of tomatoes' must be answered. What are possible challenges? What does the law say? Is there any government policy statement? Is the business sustainable?

These and similar other questions are important if one finds it profitable to remain in any activity of a value chain.

When one decides on the business option, he/she must start a company with its own specific business model, buy into a franchise with a clearly defined model or be involved in multi-level (network) marketing model. Experts say very few people make profit from network marketing. Experience, capacity, resources, interests, expectations and involvement should dictate the choice of business. Before taking action, you must do due diligence, which is an evaluation of specific elements of the business and start small at a manageable level. Above all, discuss every business plan with your spouse.

It is important to note that a business established will certainly fail and create more retirement – related problems unless you have an entrepreneurial spirit. This is essentially about self motivation, forward thinking, adequate energy and ability to take calculated risk. It also involves being creative, persistent and accepting self responsibility in your affairs. You must be passionate as great passions elevate the soul for greatness. There is strong research evidence of retiree business success. In the US for example, statistics have shown that in 2015, self employment rate among workers aged 65 and older, was higher (15.5 percent) than any other age group. *The Ewing Marion Kaufman Foundation* spoke in the same direction when it noted in its 2014 report that a quarter of all new businesses started, were owned by people aged 55 to 64.

Your business must be such that can help you experience a better work-life balance. Starting your company with its specific business model will come in the form of a sole proprietorship, partnership, a limited liability outfit or a cooperative.

(i) The sole proprietorship is owned and usually managed by the owner. The requirements for starting it are specific to the local area. It is easy to start and the expenses are low. In Nigeria, the official filing fee is Ten Thousand Naira, which is under 30 US dollars. The advantages of sole proprietorship include the fact that there are no special taxes and the profits are not shared. Also, there is the pride in the ownership and the possibility of leaving behind a legacy for the coming generation.

Sole proprietorships may be hindered by limited growth and life span. Expansion is normally slow and the business usually dies with the exit of its founder. There are also management-related difficulties as well as limited sources of finance.

(ii) Partnership is another form of business with two or more owners. There are advantages in the combination of resources just as there are possibilities of organisational disputes. It is therefore extremely advisable to document the obligations, investments and profits or losses of each partner. Unlike the sole proprietorship, there is co-ownership of assets, share in management, profit and you may be bound by the actions of any of the partners.

(iii) The limited liability company is legally separated from its owners. The owners do not have to worry about losing personal belongings due to some business problems. This kind of business enables many people to share in the ownership. Apart from the advantages of ease of ownership change, separation of ownership from management and the relative ease of raising large amount of money, it is expensive to incorporate and manage.

(iv) Franchise is the right to use a specific brand name to sell its product or service in a given location. The agreement is between the franchisor, which is the company that owns the brand and the franchisee, which is the person/company that buys a franchise. There are persons who are comfortable with joining an already established business concern than start their own from the scratch. Though very expensive, the advantages include personal ownership, tapping into an already recognised name, management and marketing assistance from the franchisor; and low rate of reported failure.

Despite the advantages, there is the possibility of dealing with a fraudulent franchisor, with attendant negative consequences and any negative market situation befalling the franchisor will certainly affect the franchisee's business. Equally, there are reported cases where management assistance turned into 'management orders', a situation a franchisor dictates for expected compliance without imputes from the franchisee.

(v) Co-operatives: *Wikipedia*, the online dictionary, defines a cooperative as 'an autonomous association of persons united voluntarily to meet their common economic, social, and cultural needs and aspirations through a jointly-owned enterprise'. The success of the consumer co-operative in Rochdale, England in 1844, which was articulated on the principles of voluntary and open membership, democratic control of members, member economic participation, autonomy and independence, co-operation between co-operatives, concern for community and training in co-operative ideals, is known to have laid the foundation for modern co-operative societies. People with needs and aspiration pull their resources together to form and own an enterprise for mutual gain. It may be consumer, housing, farming or retail cooperative. Cooperatives remain a major force in agriculture worldwide. Whatever choice a retiree decides on, he/she needs a business plan which acts as a guide to help navigate the business.

Business Plan

The essence of a plan and planning cannot be overemphasized especially in a business since many resources are involved and at various times. The idea behind the business plan expresses a carefully defined path for success. It may not necessarily determine the success but helps to avoid an impending failure.

Over the years, there has been the erroneous belief that the business plan is mainly for use in raising funds for businesses. No! This assumption may have been because it seeks to engage potential investors and financiers on an emotional level concerning their assessments of the quality of the management team as well as the entrepreneurial competence of its owners.

The business plan is beyond that. For the managers, it reveals the unknown, clarifies ideas, assists in the planning process and helps in assembling the workforce. The owners will find fulfilment in the sense that the feasibility and viability of the business will be spelt out with the capital outlay outlined as well as objectives set.

The business plan is a written document which helps in determining the essential operations of the business. It breaks the big picture into tiny details explaining why it exists and the problem it intends to solve. It decides on the issues of name, identity, key management team, product/service, its market and marketing techniques as well as industry competition. It must make sense, ensure sustainability and serve as guide for at least a year. Determining the failure of business on paper helps a prospective entrepreneur avoid waste of time, energy, resources and putting his reputation on the line.

The future direction in the business plan examines strengths, weaknesses, opportunities and threats in the business environment while the implementation issues of marketing, financial, production and human resources are also projected.

The business plan helps to avoid common pitfalls associated with previous efforts. It must be respectably short as readers are busy persons who may not have the time to go through unnecessarily lengthy documents. Figures must not be exaggerated; sufficient and verifiable details are needed and goals clearly stated. In its implementation, it can be adjusted to reflect changing circumstances.

A business plan has the following:

1. Executive Summary: This is a concise report of the entire plan stating the vision, market opportunities, key financial needs and projection and presented in a manner a reader would choose to read. It details the entire plan in a manner the reader gets a clear understanding of the fundamentals guiding the proposed business.
2. Business Description: The business description component looks at the business and its relevance to its industry and the general economy. The competition, current and future trends, and functional specification of the business are also included here.
3. Sustainability: This feature assesses the company's sustainable development strategy. Green and environmental issues are discussed in this segment.

4. Marketing: This component analyses the market niche and share, competitive analysis, marketing strategies and policy fundamentals as well as advertising plans.
5. Operations: This aspect of the plan details the process, technology, proximity to suppliers, transport and logistics plan
6. Financials: Issues of financial component include balance sheet, cash flow statements and sales information presented in a professional manner.
7. The Risk Analysis Segment anticipates uncertainties in the market and provides alternative course(s) of action.
8. Harvest Strategy: This segment deals with issues relating to shares transfer, succession plan and investor exit strategy.
9. Milestone Schedule highlights the planned duration of events which may be in weeks or months needed to implement major activities like feasibility investigation, approval by promoters, incorporation. Accounts and initial funding, employment of key staff, site preparation, preparation of plant and office, equipment installation, test-running of facilities and commissioning of plant, among others.

Frederick, O'Connor and Kuratko[6] have given a useful detailed guide for developing a business plan.

1. Executive Summary:
   - No more than three pages. This is the most crucial part of your plan because you must capture the reader's interest.
   - What, how, why, where and so on must be summarised
   - Complete this part after you have a finished business plan
2. Business Description Segment

- The name of your business

- A background of the industry with history of your company should be covered here
- The potential of the new venture should be described clearly
- Any uniqueness or distinctive features of this venture should be clearly described

3. Sustainability
   - Craft a definition of sustainable development that is specific to your firm and that can serve as a guidepost for business conduct.
4. Marketing Segment
   - Convince investors that sales projections and competition can be met
   - Use and disclose market studies
   - Identify target market, market position and market share
   - Evaluate all competition and specifically cover why and how you will be better than your competitors
   - Identify all market sources and assistance used for this segment
   - Demonstrate pricing strategy since your price must penetrate and maintain a market share to produce profits
5. Operations Segment
   - Describe the advantages of your location. List the production needs in terms of facilities (plant, storage, office space) and equipment (machinery, furniture, supplies).
   - Describe the access to transportation
   - Indicate proximity to your suppliers
   - Mention the availability of labour in your location
6. Sustainability Development measures of Performance

- Simply ask, 'How do we meet the needs of the present without compromising the ability of future generations to meet their own needs?'
- 'Do stakeholders raise sustainability issues about the firm?'
- Explain the process your firm might implement to reasonably estimate sustainability impacts, risks and opportunities.

7. Management Segment
   - Supply resumes of all key people in the management of your venture
   - Carefully describe the legal structure of your venture
   - Cover the added assistance of advisors, consultants and directors
   - Give information on how and how much everyone is to be compensated.
8. Financial Segment
   - Give actual estimated statement
   - Describe the needed sources for your funds and the uses you intend for the money
   - Develop and present a budget
   - Create stages of financing for purposes of allowing evaluation by investors at various points
9. Critical-risks Segment
   - Discuss Potential risk before investors point them out – for example; Price cutting by competitors; any potential unfavourable industry-wide trends; Physical, regulatory or reputational risks due to climate change; Design or manufacturing costs in excess of estimates; Sales projection not achieved; provide some alternative causes of action.

10. Harvest Strategy Segment
    - Outline a plan for the orderly transfer of company assets
    - Describe the plan for transition of leadership
    - Mention the preparations needed for the continuity of the business
11. Milestone Schedule Segment
    - Develop a timetable or chart to demonstrate when each phase of the venture is to be completed.

Your business plan may not be as comprehensive or may not use the template as highlighted but, you should be well guided. You may even know entrepreneurs that succeed without business plan. Timing, entrepreneurial drive, environmental factors and luck may have favoured them but, chances are greater they will fail. In as much as a business plan does not guarantee success, it remains one of the ways to help you succeed.

In the choice of workers, employ only persons with relevant skills and those you can sack should the need arise. Relatives may not always fit into the suggested category of staff to employ. Dispensing with their services in an event of misconduct may bring *bad blood* within the family.

I would like to end this chapter on an advisory note. Business ethics are very important in business and should be coveted. They are standards for proper business conduct and behaviour. They are the principles and standards with which an organisation deals with its stakeholders and environmental issues when they arise. Ethics provide the moral compass for a business and ensure a sustainable goodwill. They help create good corporate image and positive work culture. You should therefore embrace gender, religious and cultural diversities. Confidentiality of your dealings with clients is important, honest earnings must be emphasised just as promises are kept. You need to know your work, show commitment, take care of your people, expect positive results and be happy. The assurance of a meaningful retirement can only be guaranteed in well-planned and implemented value-added consistent activities.

CHAPTER SIX

INDEPENDENT LIFE AS A CONSULTANT

> *A strong and well-constituted man digests his experiences (deeds and misdeeds all included) just as he digests his meat, even when he has some tough morsels to swallow.* Ralph Waldo Emerson

'George Gordon Battle Liddy, known as G. Gordon Liddy, is a former FBI Agent, Lawyer, Talk Show Host, Actor and prominent figure in the Watergate scandal as the Chief Operative in the White House Plumbers Unit during the Nixon Administration. Liddy was convicted of conspiracy, burglary and illegal wiretapping for his role in the scandal… which led to the Nixon's resignation in 1974' – Wikipedia.

Right after he got out of prison, Mr Liddy commanded a six figure income as a Consultant from his experience-related engagement. The above scenario explains how even a seemingly unpleasant situation can turn one into becoming a consultant. Consulting is based on an individual's unique experience and readiness to share experience for a fee. It does not require much capital to start.

Consulting has remained a very big industry with some estimates indicating $400billion in just human capital in business. Consulting is the provision of a third party professional or semi professional service to a client for a fee. Consultants operate in all fields of endeavours: health, export, human resource, marketing, engineering, education, government service and accounting are the more common ones.

Consulting is different from coaching. Consulting is described by *Wikipedia*, the online dictionary as a relationship which is designed and defined in a relationship between client and a coach. It is based on the clients expressed interest, goals and objectives. The two concepts are different even though their services overlap.

While coaching helps individuals within an organisation on one-on-one basis, the Consultant is usually engaged by the organisation. The coaching – client relationship is frequent and interactive as against the minimal and not so often interaction of the Consultant and the client. The Consultants are hired for specific problem and cease operations once a solution is given. The Coach on the other hand, is appointed on a long term purpose. The client of the Consultants receives information hitherto not available whereas the Coach needs available information in accomplishing his/her task. It was estimated by a 2016 global coaching study sponsored by the International Coaching Federation and Price Waterhouse Coopers (PWC) that there are more than 53,300 professional Coaches worldwide and 54% are aged 50+. It is apparent that consulting is not only for the young.

When do we need Consultants?

Consultancy services may be required for the following reasons:

i. For Efficiency: Inefficiency shrinks performance and increases the cost of business operations. Organisations experiencing loss of market position, increasing cost of business operations and continued supply deficiencies may require the services of a Consultant to help improve efficiency in the affected areas.

ii. Research and data processing: I know of a fellow who makes a decent living through the provision of computer and data analysis for students. The computer skills which enable him the easy use of different statistical packages keep him in a position of a Consultant whose services are required.

iii. Government regulations: Certain programmes and projects mandatorily require the services of Consultants. Road construction for example requires the provision of an Environmental Impact Assessment (EIA) before its commencement. Also, it is mandatory for external auditors to peruse organisation's books of account before they are published. Such responsibilities are given to Consultants with cognate experience.

iv. Company politics: Sometimes, events play out in an organisation where the management knows the truth but for office politics, shift the responsibility to a Consultant to deliver the verdict. On the other hand, an organisation may need the services of a Consultant as an independent assessor to affirm or reject a proposal, strategy or programme.

v. Marketing services: Marketing remains one of the most important activities of business as it brings product or service to its user. Most organisations have issues with low market position or lack of information about their competitor or market. A Consultant may be needed in this regard. I remember having issues with the marketing of my Television programme on Enterprise Development which persisted until I consulted a professional.

vi. Computer and internet service: This is a multi-billion dollar business that has spanned every facet of the economy - whether in hard or software applications - consulting expertise is needed. The Corona virus pandemic has further expanded this service profile.

vii. Complete Turnaround: The business environment is so dynamic that the strategy adopted the day before may not fit into the system of contemporary times. The process, model and even the product or service may require a recalibration or total turnaround where experts will be needed on consultancy basis. An exposure to a particular environment may just do the magic. William Brandt of Development Specialist Incorporated for instance became a Consultant while studying for his doctorate degree. A friend invited him to assist a failing coal mine and ever since then, Mr Brandt has remained a renowned Consultant.

viii. Training Needs: Training needs occur in almost all activities of business: new technology, updating of skills, fresh ideas, new responsibilities, leadership and various other activities of business. Even when organisations have their training unit, they still collaborate with Consultants to accomplish their tasks.

ix. Personnel Needs: Sometimes certain key activities of an organisation are given out to Consultants for a brief period of time. This may happen when specific tasks or unique skills are needed at short notice. Consultants are equally used for employment purposes during the recruitment of new staff.

x. Need to raise funds: The ubiquitous role of money has further raised the need for Consultants to be used in this regard. They may come in as financial advisers, in the writing of business plan, for legal and auditing services, among others.
xi. Ecommerce: The global ecommerce market valued at over 9 trillion dollars with expected growth rate of about 15% between 2020 and 2027 indicate availability of opportunities for interested persons.

To be a Consultant, one must be endowed with management skills which should help in converting diverse experiences, talents and knowledge into a business endeavour. This includes the ability to identify specific interest areas as well as develop marketing and sales strategy for business ideas. Communication skills as well as the analytical ability to diagnose problems and proffer solutions are equally very important.

Good communication is a two-way relationship. The most effective exchange of information happens when both the good sender and good listener are involved. Being a good listener leads to deeper understanding of the issues involved, shows respect and helps ensure accurate perceptions. Technical expertise and knowledge are the distinguishing elements that determine the area of operation which could be accounting, computing, research or whatever option one may consult in.

Having worked for a while, there are experiences, ideas, information and innovations one can transfer which would be useful and engaging. Such ideas may draw relevance from your former work or is developed through interaction with your environment. Using it to proffer a solution to people may elevate your relevance in retirement even more than when you were working.

Stories of how people became Consultants

(1) Name:	Kim Lopez-Walters, 43[7]
Previous position:	Consumer Strategist at the market research
Current position:	New Product Consultant to the food and beverage industry

How she got her start:

After being laid off in July 2008, Lopez-Walters decided to use her decades of experience working for brands such as Pepsi, Quaker Oats, Nestle, Starbucks, and PowerBar to launch her own consulting practice, emphasizing her extensive background in new product development: "That's my specialty," she says. "I know how to launch and reposition food products." Fortunately, Lopez-Walters had carefully cultivated her network of past coworkers and employers — many of whom ended up providing her with her first opportunities and referrals.

How she's doing:

"So far it's been great," says Lopez-Walters, adding that she has no desire to return to the traditional workforce since the consulting lifestyle fits her needs as the mother of three young girls. One thing that's secured her a steady stream of work has been her recent discovery of an interesting niche — taking over projects for employees who are going out on family or maternity leave. That's helped her generate an income about 30 percent higher than her previous full-time salary. "But with my new expenses — office, insurance, health care, and taxes — it really becomes a wash," she says. The real upside? The increased freedom and flexibility that comes with managing her own schedule.

Complications:

Her biggest concern is income security. "I'm banking away as much as I can in case projects dry up," says Lopez-Walters. "That's the risk consultants always have in the back of their head." Things are even more pressing now: Just as her business was hitting its stride, her husband was laid off from his full-time position, making her the sole breadwinner. It's anxiety-provoking, but she's confident they'll get through it. Her husband, meanwhile, has had the opportunity to spend more time with the kids.

(2)Name:	Grant Son, 45[7]
Previous Position:	Vice President of consumer marketing, Time Inc.
Current Position:	Consultant to new and established interactive media companies

How he got his start:

Son, whose career in media has spanned nearly 25 years, was laid off last December when Time Inc. cut a third of its consumer marketing staff. As it happened, Son had already been considering a return to the entrepreneurial fray (he'd been CEO of a publishing startup that was eventually acquired by ESPN), and he decided to pursue consulting rather than jump into another full-time job commitment to give him time to develop and launch his new company. Getting his first projects wasn't hard. "I've worked for the top brands in the business," says Son, so he was able to generate plenty of work just from former colleagues. Right after he got laid off, Son sent a mass email about his consulting practice to his entire social network, and some of his ex-colleagues at Time Inc. immediately responded with offers of work ranging from web design to business development, which Son and his "virtual team" were happy to accept.

<u>How he's doing</u>:

Surprisingly well. As Son points out, one side effect of the economic climate is the huge amount of recently displaced talent on the streets, available for work as part of a "virtual" team. "I've been able to enlist many former business associates as part of my network, which allows me to offer a comprehensive set of services," he says. "We can basically do everything needed to run a new media company, from marketing and development to operations and finance." As a result, Son's been able to present a much bigger portfolio of options to his clients — resulting in an income that has so far run about 20 percent ahead of his prior salary.

<u>Complications:</u>

Son always saw consulting as bridge toward his real priority — his new startup. As client work mounted, though, he realized he needed to start shifting time and attention out of his consulting practice and into his startup venture. His solution: He struck a deal with one of his clients to barter his skills and experience as "entrepreneur in residence" in exchange for the office space, infrastructure, and services he'll need to get his venture going. He's begun to cut back his client load in preparation for launch, which he says is on track for sometime in the next year. "In the coming months, things will improve to the point where companies are seeking out new opportunities," Son says. "And by that time, I'll be ready to go public with the details of my new venture."

(3)Name: David Mark, 57[7]
Previous position: R&D Scientist
Current position: Nutritional marketing consultant

How he got his start:

Mark, who has a Ph.D. in Nutritional Biochemistry, was an R&D scientist for two decades, working for companies such as Monsanto, and most recently, Welch's Grape Juice. He cites "bad weather" as the reason for being laid off from Welch's in 2004: Welch's only has three growing regions in the entire United States, and two of the three went sour in one year. The result was staff cuts across the board. Realizing that at age 52, he was probably "two jobs away from retirement," he turned to consulting as a way to bring his career in for a "soft landing." Welch's ended up being his very first client. Mark knew that the research project he'd been working on at the time of his lay-off still needed to be wrapped up, so he offered to do it as a consultant, and his former boss readily agreed. Additional jobs came from other former employers of Mark's.

How he's doing:

Mark's specialty is discerning whether science supports health claims — and, as consumer interest in healthy foods and beverages rises, he's found himself ideally positioned to benefit. "My overhead is minimal, my business is steady, and I'm making more than I would have been if I'd stayed salaried," says Mark, who's satisfied that he's made the right choice.

Complications:

Probably the biggest concern on Mark's mind is avoiding complacency. In order to avoid taking his success for granted, every year, on the anniversary of launching his practice, Mark takes time off to do "strategic planning," thinking about how better to grow and position his business. He's also rigorous about self-discipline. "I make sure I always put in a full workday; if things slow down, I work on writing articles for industry and consumer health magazines," something he says is an important way to stay top of mind with clients and prospects. "My only curse is that my office is too near the refrigerator," he says.

(4)Name: Paul Uduk, 62
Previous position: Senior Bank Manager
Current position: Business Consultant/Coach

Paul Uduk is the founder and CEO at Vision & Talent Group, providing insight and skills for today's business. A trainer par excellence, he is also a highly sought-after Public Speaker. Paul loves writing. He is a Platinum Author at Ezine Articles, made up of about 500,000 expert authors. He has written for Process Excellence Network (PEX), comprising 160,000 process practitioners from all over the world. Paul is the author of 7 books, including *Bridges to the Customer's Heart*, dubbed the Customer Service Bible. Paul and his Vision & Talent Group have trained some of the biggest institutions and brands you know, including Fortune 500 companies, Nestle, Heineken (Nigerian Breweries), Dangote, First Bank, Nestoil (whose clients include ExxonMobil, Shell, Chevron, Total-Elf, Eni and Nigerian National Petroleum Company(NNPC). Others are Honeywell, Berger, Techno Oil, Access (Diamond), AccessPFC, DiamondPFC, Fidelity, Ecobank, First City Monument Bank, Polaris, Leadway Assurance, Linkage Insurance, Sovereign Trust, Anchor, Smile, Inlaks Computers, Cowry, Nigeria Deposit Insurance Corporation, Bank of Industry, CR Services, Central Securities Clearing System, Securities & Exchange Commission, ISN Medical,

Teknokleen, Vibrant, Infinity, Bosak, and Greensprings Schools, amongst others.

Paul has delivered customized keynote presentations at conferences and seminars organized by institutions such as UNDP, Institute of Chartered Sales Professionals, Institute of Management Consultants, Chartered Institute of Personnel Management, Full Circle Wellness Solution, GMYT, Chartered Institute of Bankers of Nigeria and Informa (one of the world's largest training and expo groups), among others. He is passionately involved in guiding people to write bestseller books. In his words 'as an author, you enter the immortality'. Paul has made these achievements after retirement from a banking career in 2010. He had worked for 27 years in the banking sector.

CHAPTER SEVEN

WOULDN'T YOU RATHER FARM!

This time, like all times, is a very good one, if we but know what to do with it. Ralph Waldo Emerson

There are agricultural opportunities for retirees. Agriculture plays a vital role in creating wealth in the national economy. It provides food and raw materials, creates effective demand, helps during depression by providing basic necessities of life, brings in foreign exchange and it is a veritable source of employment, In Nigeria, agriculture provides the main source of livelihood, employing two thirds of the entire workforce. But, production challenges have stifled its performance leaving room for large scale importation of food into the country. The novel Corona virus pandemic which restricted movements and shrunk credits has further expressed additional challenges on the agriculture landscape.

The gap in production has therefore provided an ample opportunity for interested investors in the sector. The Food and Agriculture Organisation predicts a $1 trillion market in the African sub-Saharan region by 2030. For the retiree, the relatively low risk associated with agriculture and its income-generating propensity can be engaging and avert a sedentary lifestyle. The gradual agricultural process from planting through tendering to harvesting can equally help in health maintenance in retirement. Agricultural activities include feeds dealership, farm inputs supply, raw and processed food marketing, produce storage, equipment hiring and in recent times, greenhouse cultivation which enables the farmer to maximise the use of scarce resources for optimum yield. Opportunities which exist in specific areas are here discussed.

i. Cassava Production and Processing:

Cassava remains one of the most important staple foods in West Africa. Varieties include those which are high in starch content, high *garri* index, diseases resistant and early maturity, among others. Cassava can be processed into various forms such as alcohol, starch, *garri* and pellets. I understand cassava flour may be used in baking bread.

ii. Fish Farming:

Fish remains a reliable source of animal protein which is rich in minerals, vitamins and lipids. Food and Agriculture Organisation (FAO) figures indicate that Nigeria is a net importer of fish with the value of USD 1.2 billion in 2013. More than 80% of local fish production is generated at the artisan small-scale level hence a dominant market for fish farming which is popular, lucrative and without environmental hazard. Fish farming does not require much space.

iii. Poultry Farming:

Poultry or domesticated bird farming is arguably the fastest growing farming in Nigerian agricultural sector. Its lean meat, egg production and manure are easily marketable and affordable for all. With an estimated Nigerian population of one hundred and eighty million persons, there is a large daily market for the products. Chicken grow very fast maturing within few weeks. With a relatively low capital, one can engage in layer-breading for egg production, broiler rearing for meat, be involved in feeds distribution or settle for the more expensive and technologically advanced hatchery, for the production of new chicks.

iv. Cocoa Farming

Cocoa, though native to South America, has most of its modern day production in West African region. Apart from its nutritional and medicinal values, its by-product is useful in the confectionery industry and its seed remains a major ingredient in chocolate production. Cocoa is traded on the global commodity market.

v. Piggery

Pig farming is a game changer when compared to other domesticated animals. With a relatively shorter reproduction cycle, it has a quicker rate of returns on investment. Other advantages are in its use in research endeavours, good source for leather production; efficient utilisation of table garbage, unmarketable grains and vegetables as its feed, and in the production of pork, bacon and ham. About 1.7 tonnes of pork meat was imported into Nigeria in 2017. Tridge, the global trade platform reported that lard import for the same year was USD 10.2 million. Lard is the fat from the abdomen of pigs.

vi. Grass-cutter Farming:

The aggressive hunting of this rodent due to land development has threatened its existence thus encouraging its domestication for economic reasons. Its popularity may be linked to its quality meat and with no cultural or religious restrictions. Grass-cutters are farmed naturally with no growth stimulants and chemicals fed to them hence the high demand for the meat. They could be farmed within residential areas as they have no offensive smell and would not make noise.

vii. Rabbit Production:

The small body-sized, easy to manage, disease resistant and high fertility rodent has high quality, tender and nutritious meat. Apart from its high protein content, it is in high demand in research and experimental purposes. It is economically viable to engage in its farming.

viii. Snail Farming:

Snail meat is fat and cholesterol free and it is more nutritious than chicken. It is rich in protein, iron, calcium, magnesium and vitamin A. Snails are in high demand and the farming requires low capital and intensity. Farming in snail is equally lucrative.

ix. Maize Farming:

Maize is a major cereal crop in West Africa. Its caloric supply of 19% is the world's highest, supplying more calorie than rice at 16.5% and wheat at 15%. Maize which is an all-season grain is used as a meal and for industrial use by flour millers, animal feed manufacturers and confectionery makers.

x. Oil Palm Farming

Transplanted palm mature and bear fruits in about 4 years. Native to West Africa, it has successfully thrived in Asian countries particularly Malaysia. Its component parts are of value to different persons. Brooms are obtained from the rib of the leaf, timber from the stem, roots serve as manure, the seed is processed for oil and cake, branches for tent construction and basket making, and the shell is a source of fuel. Palm oil and palm kernel oils are consumed and are among the world's most versatile raw materials. Asides its long gestation period before seed bearing and the large expanse of land needed for its cultivation, it may be one of the most suited engagements for the retiree in the environment which favours its planting.

xi. Floriculture:

House and city beautification is fast making floriculture popular. Residential, commercial and religious buildings are usually adorned with this gift of nature for unique appearance, elegance and serenity. Flowers are among the most profitable plants with high yielding economic value. Kenya's flower export is worth over USD 750 million annually. Beside those discussed, farming opportunities worth exploiting in retirement also include cattle rearing, bee keeping and mushroom cultivation.

CHAPTER EIGHT

THE STRESS FACTOR

I thought the stress of work would kill me; now I am afraid the boredom of retirement will. Anonymous

The online medical dictionary, *MedlinePlus,* defines stress as 'a feeling of emotional or physical tension. It can come from any event or thought that makes you feel frustrated, angry, or nervous'. It is related to the mind and intellectual power. It is the body's reaction to positive or negative life situations. A positive stress keeps you alert and conscious to challenge an impending situation. It is a defence-generated preparedness that leaves immediately the situation is over.

For the retiree, the positive stress may come during the pre-retirement planning period. This is a period of anxiety as to what retirement would bring. Questions bordering on life in retirement will cause unsettled moments. Have I planned enough? Will my entitlements be paid or delayed? Will my savings be adequate? This kind of tension goes off on retirement.

On the other hand, the negative stress is that which continues without a relief. It has the tendency to express itself as mental slide, depression and is capable of distorting the normal flow of the body chemistry. It places a major challenge on the retiree's health and disrupts emotional balance. Experts say it comes with health challenges like headaches, insomnia, upset stomach, elevated blood pressure, sex dysfunction, memory loss, poor regulation of emotions and chest pain. It is commonly referred to as a slow killer.

For the retiree, the negative stress may come as one faces the actual retirement, unprepared. Situations like relishing the fancy and fantasy of former office now occupied by someone else, staying indoors without any plans for the next day, not having the company of right acquaintances or suffering from any misfortune in silence. The London-based Institute of Economic Affairs is of the opinion that there is a 40% probability of depression upon retirement. A life story of negative stress is as given below as reported in *The Guardian* of London on April 25, 2017:

> Ageism at work: 'As a female presenter, I was replaced by younger models'
>
> I am in my late 50s and have worked as a journalist for nearly 30 years, both on-screen as a reporter and off-screen as a news producer. I used to love my job and felt like a valued member of the team. Sadly, that has changed over the last 10 years.
>
> I still have knowledge, looks and talent but I do not fit the media stereotype
>
> I am denied opportunities given to younger members of staff and sidelined by managers, despite having the knowledge and experience to cover the story. I constantly volunteer for news projects but am not included in the team and made to feel invisible. I have to help far less experienced journalists do a job that I am being denied the opportunity to do, which is

frustrating. This is especially the case when I have to save them from making legal or factual mistakes. This is all because the bosses prefer to have younger reporters on screen. They would not consider having a woman over 50 on camera. I still have knowledge, looks and talent but I do not fit the media stereotype.

In the morning news meetings if I offer my opinion on something I am often cut off mid sentence or completely dismissed. I have tried to ignore this, but it has chipped away at my confidence and now I don't bother to voice my opinions or bring ideas to the table for fear of being made to look stupid.

For the last few years I have not been given the same training and promotional opportunities as younger members of staff. It is as if my career has stopped. This is crazy because now I have time to commit more to work and do longer shifts as my family are all grown up and have left home. With state pensions not being available until 67, I now have to work longer and I want to feel fulfilled at work. Something I seem unable to get across to management, despite numerous conversations.

When I try to highlight the issue of ageism with younger female members of staff, they say it is not a big problem. However, I have watched these same people change their minds 10 years down the line when they are taken off screen to be replaced by a younger model and their voices are not heard any more. What's even more frustrating is that at the same time older, male journalists are being left to carry on reporting on screen.

Outside work, I am confident and articulate and have achieved many things. But in work I feel constantly degraded and humiliated by ageist comments. Mistakes I make are highlighted and the response to those mistakes is totally disproportionate, but when younger members of staff make the same mistakes it is brushed aside. I have to defend myself against fabricated allegations that are used to undermine my credibility in the workplace. I have seen this happen to older friends of mine who eventually could not carry on with the stress of the situation and took early retirement.

I am left with the feeling that my only option is to leave and find another job. But in my late 50s that is easier said than done. And there is the added feeling of anger: why should I be forced out of a job that I am good at just because I am seen as too old?

All this is starting to affect my mental and physical health. I am nervous, tearful and do not sleep properly. I am constantly rehearsing conversations I want to have with management to stop this ageist behaviour towards me. I get up in the morning with a feeling of dread because I know I will be subjected to ageist comments and have no way of defending myself.

When I see my boss in the office my heart is racing and I feel nervous as I await the next onslaught of criticism. I fear it will make me cry, which only goes to make me look more like an old woman who cannot cope with the stress of a busy newsroom.

Stress Management

The 2008 Gale Encyclopaedia of Medicine defines stress management as 'set of techniques and programs intended to help people deal effectively with stress and their lives by analysing the specific stressors and taking positive actions to minimise their effects'. Managing stress will help you to overcome the pressure and challenges associated with it therefore, allowing you to take control. It is not weakness to look for help among professionals. Wouldn't you rather visit the mechanic, for an example than lose your car?

The foundation for stress management may be traced to the 1967 work of Thomas Holmes and Richard Rahe which studied how stress contributes to ailments. They investigated 5000 medical patients and the work resulted in the identification of 43 life events/items and corresponding stress scores:

Events/Activities	Scores
Death of a spouse	100
Divorce	73
Marital separation	65
Imprisonment	63
Death of a close family member	63
Personal injury or illness	53
Marriage	50
Dismissal from work	47
Marital reconciliation	45
Retirement	45

Change in health of family member	44
Pregnancy	40
Sexual difficulties	39
Gain a new family member	39
Business readjustment	39
Change in financial state	38
Death of a close friend	37
Change to different line of work	36
Change in frequency of arguments	35
Major mortgage	32
Foreclosure of mortgage or loan	30
Change in responsibilities at work	29
Child leaving home	29
Trouble with in-laws	29
Outstanding personal achievement	28
Spouse starts or stops work	26
Beginning or end of school	26
Change in living conditions	25
Revision of personal habits	24
Trouble with boss	23
Change in working hours or conditions	20
Change in residence	20
Change in schools	20
Change in recreation	19
Change in church activities	19
Change in social activities	18
Minor mortgage or loan	17
Change in sleeping habits	16
Change in number of family reunions	15
Change in eating habits	15
Vacation	13
Major Holiday	12
Minor violation of law	11

Score of 300 and above:	High risk of illness.
Score of 150-299:	Moderate risk of illness
Score of less than 150:	Probability of slight risk of illness.

Figure 2: Holmes and Rahe Stress Table

Looking at the stress Table, you will agree that retirement can cause over 300 points mark of the most stressful items which are likely to happen at the same time. Imagine for example, someone retiring at the same time with the spouse who has been taken ill of a terminal disease and they have their children in school. Meanwhile, the person is living in a rented apartment and has a pension entitlement which certainly is lower than salary received while working. It would be a miracle for the fellow to escape a serious sickness.

Solutions to Stress:

1. Identify the source of your stress by closely looking at your habits, attitudes and excuses. Ask questions like: What caused it? What was my response? What did I do to feel better?
2. Learn to accept the things you cannot change, avoid the ones you can and learn to forgive (even yourself) and move on.
3. Practice an exercise which can douse the tension.
4. Reach out to a trusted, dependable and knowledgeable friend, professional or colleague
5. Set aside daily relaxation time and be involved in something that makes you laugh.
6. Time management is of essence.
7. Keep a healthy lifestyle.
8. Lower alcohol, sugar and caffeine intake and avoid self medication.
9. Good sleep is very important.
10. Spend about one hour daily reading something of interest.
11. Engage in regular meditation and other spiritual activities.

CHAPTER NINE

HEALTH MATTERS

How far you go in life depends on your being tender with the young, compassionate with the aged, sympathetic with the striving, and tolerant of the weak and strong. Because someday in your life you will have been all of these. George Washington Carver

Health is the state of complete physical, mental, emotional and social wellbeing. It is everybody's life expectation and the most priceless asset of life. But, as you grow older, it is expected that there will be certain changes in the body due to ageing which will certainly affect the health. The skin will be thicker with noticeable wrinkles and spots, the bone density will shrink in mass and become weaker, joints will be inflamed and painful, and there may be altered curvature of the back vertebrae. The teeth may be weak and brittle, just as the immune system will get weaker. There may be sleep disorder, memory problems, blurred vision and incontinence associated with bladder weakness.

Hippocrates, the father of modern medicine, is known to have said that 'health is the greatest of human blessings'. Your health and wealth are closely related. Without health, it is easy to deplete one's savings, live in assisted life and become a concern for loved ones.

Good health matters so much in meaningful retirement. Regular checkups to prevent disease and tooth decay are by far more cost effective than attending to them at an advanced stage.

The attitude you adopt in retirement has a major influence. Is it a negative attitude of regrets, sadness, anxiety or bitterness? Then, you will be prone to having fears, feeling inferior to others, criticising often and blaming others for your circumstances. Your relationship with people will certainly falter.

A rather positive attitude admits strength, vigour, growth and success. Life takes on us as our mind creates it. Remember 'as a man thinketh, so is he'. Your perception of retirement can bring either self confidence with attendant radiant disposition to health or a defeatist and sullen mentality which hinders good health.

Retirement will certainly affect the lifestyle. So how is your health? You may not have been conscious of the state of your health but, it is not late. Be comforted with the Chinese saying 'the best time to have planted a tree was 20 years ago; the second best time is now'. Therefore, start taking serious the things that pertain to your health.

1. Medically determine your health status. Feeling fine does not indicate a good health. There are cases of people who died in their sleep and were fine the previous day, or collapsed while performing a normal routine assignment. There is need to have a medical examination to ascertain the true health condition. Such an examination guides future life pattern. You may be hypertensive, diabetic or having other ailments common with people of 50 years and above. Such medical conditions are medically diagnosed.
2. Expect that things may not necessarily go the way you had planned. Plans are good but they are based on uncertainties

you may not control. In as much as you plan to succeed, leave room for the unexpected. This will help lower the impact of an unexpected outcome, especially if it is negative.

3. Eat well. Diet is a personal thing and should be pleasurable. Some food suggestions which are good for some may not be good for others. Eating well is not about the quantity, but regular healthy meals suitable for the individual. Certain meals may not be convenient but, fruits, oats, vegetables and clean water are generally recommended just as sugar, alcohol, red meat and dairy milk reduction is commonly advised.
4. Be part of your community through giving. What are you giving back to your community? You can serve in your local church or mosque, organise free lessons, be involved in charity or be engaged in free counselling service and many more.

Giving gives a feeling of joy and fulfilment and it is good for health. Stephen Post, a Professor of Preventive Medicine and Jill Neimark in their book *Why Good Things Happen to Good People*, report that giving increases health benefits in people including those with chronic diseases like HIV. Affirming the claim, scientists at the Institute of HeartMath in California, have also shown that gratitude reduces stress hormones and boosts immunity.

Giving promotes cooperation, evokes gratitude and is contagious; it spurs ripple effects of generosity throughout the community. So, give even if it is your old books, there are libraries, your old clothes, electronics and furniture. There are people that need them. Give and be healthy.

1. Be physically active. Physical exercise helps the heart, reduces the risk of dementia and is known to produce endorphins

which are a mood booster to the health. Exercise prevents disease and helps in its management. It is also a good source of social engagement.

2. Be focused. Make a list of daily activities and allocate time accordingly. Accomplishing these daily tasks has the ability to satisfy and give you a sense of accomplishment and further motivation.
3. Fight loneliness as much as you can. Scientists at Brigham Young University have successfully shown loneliness and social isolation as major mortality factor.
4. Renew your mind with constant reading. Reading produces energy, frees the mind and releases the hygiene to cleanse it from toxins.
5. Gradual settlement: you must acknowledge the need for a transition from career to a new life in retirement. Organise, plan and moderate your activities and expenditures to reflect the new status.
6. Researchers at Maryland University say people that watch more television are generally less happy than those that watch less, so watch less of it.
7. Ask questions and seek clarity when confused and be prepared to give honest answers when questions are directed at you. Honesty calms the mind and stops adrenaline anxiety.
8. Good sleep reduces stress, refreshes and enhances the health. Sleep is known to prevent cancer, improve memory, helps to keep alert and nourishes the heart. New studies have identified insomnia as the underlying signs of an impending sickness. Emily Francos admonishes thus: 'my only relief is sleep. When I am asleep, I am not sad, I am not angry, I am not lonely, I am nothing'. Give yourself a good sleep.

9. When diagnosed with an ailment, take the drugs as recommended by the medics. The internet may be rich in ideas, yet, avoid medical treatments recommended on the net.
10. Above all, spoil yourself once in a while. There is only one life and you are the centre of it. Remember, 'if you do not make time for your wellness, you will be forced to make time for your illnesses' and the hope for a meaningful retirement will be negatively affected, so always remember to treat yourself fine.

CHAPTER TEN

PERSONAL FINANCE

Money is like a sixth sense-and you can't make use of the other five without it.
Somerset Maugham

Personal finance is the management of the individual or family level financial issues as they affect the income, consumption, investment and savings. Income refers to inflows like salaries, wages, dividends, and pensions. Consumptions come in the forms of expenditures on food, rent, taxes, car purchases and repairs, utilities, and healthcare, among others. In terms of retirement expenditure, allocation for clothing for instance may be substantially reduced compared to work-time days.

Investments are those purchases with a promised return on invested money and an added profit over a period of time. Savings may refer to excess cash set aside for future spending and may include bank deposits. In retirement income generally comes from occupational and State functions, personal savings and investments, donations and social benefits. Depending entirely on the State for income is not healthy. Since such amounts are fixed, they may be meaningless over time. A friend of mine for instance was comfortable with his monthly retirement take-home pay of ₦14,000 in 2010, the same amount of money could not pay his electricity and phone recharge bills in 2020. Be wise!

Financial Stages of Life

The individual has five financial stages of life which affect the personal finance function in different ways. At the *early career stage,* life starts as a young worker with attention for survival and basic needs of life. Wealth accumulation begins here. Planning for the future looks so far off at this stage as attention is more on the present, but this is the best stage for financial education which most people are ignorant of. The *career progression* is the wealth management stage which comes with retirement consciousness, family responsibility, investments and house ownership. Moonlighting is highly encouraged at this stage to make ends meet. At the *pre-retirement stage,* debt issues would have been seriously reduced, the children are on their way out of school and investment portfolios have grown. This stage is the beginning of wealth distribution. The *early retirement stage* would have presented a clearer picture of the finance structure in retirement with the *later retirement stage* optimizing investments against inflation, taxes and losses.

Setting and achieving personal finance goals for a meaningful retirement depend on how one manages his personal finance. Countless authors, philosophers and academics have written and counselled on this. While their books and stories are worthy and inspiring, none can adequately capture the unique circumstances and experiences each of us face in making financial decisions. They essentially generalise.

In as much as there is no magic formula that suits everyone, you must certainly have a retirement investment portfolio at all times which you must consistently reinvest for a sustainable lifetime income. The aim is to produce investment returns that meet yearly inflation-adjusted living expenses while preserving the value of the portfolio. This will enable you strike a balance between expected returns, and desired standard of living. In doing so, you must realise that investment, consumption and expenditure patterns change according to retirement plan horizon. For instance, a person with many years before retirement may be comfortable with an investment in stocks. This is because though volatile, stocks have historically outperformed other securities over long time periods. This may explain the enormous wealth of Warren Buffet, an American billionaire, who has been investing in stocks for about a quarter of a century but started making his millions after about 60 years of age.

But, for those about to retire, less volatile securities that promise more income to live on may be the preferred option. But, in all, a mixture of short and long-term investments is recommended. The advantages are many. For instance, just as it may take weeks or months to sale a landed property or a particular period to end a treasury bill transaction, stocks can easily be converted to cash in a moment of cash emergency.

One major way of achieving personal finance goals, no matter our circumstances, backgrounds, needs and desires, is through budgeting. Budgeting is the process of setting financial plans and allocating specific resources based on revenue expectations. It is limiting the overall use of resources on specified units/activities. A budget helps one to stay within his/her resources by trimming down unnecessary expenses and focusing on important and critical needs. Normally, people spend as much as the resources are available and even borrow to spend. Spending without budgeting cannot place you on a scale of evaluating if you are achieving your financial goals or not. Since other factors including inflation can affect the inflow of resources, a budget helps in directing expenses to areas of greater importance. Budgeting works if you are honest about your income and expenditure hence proper budgeting and its implementation can bring peace of mind.

Family budget may fail to achieve its purpose if members are not working as a team. You must therefore carry your spouse along in the budgeting process. A divided focus can be detrimental. Family budget may fail if you do not keep track or adequately estimate the cost of your expenditure. You will end up either overestimating or underestimating the costs. Besides, you must avoid the temptation of lumping needs and wants together. They must be separated to enable an adjustment if planned expenditure overshoots the expected income. It is advisable to include all expenditure items no matter the size just as it is wrong to assume that your monthly bills are fixed and non-negotiable. Since you are the centrepiece of activities, you must also budget for periodic fun. You may end up spending more if not budgeted for. It is equally important to budget for an emergency like unplanned medical attention.

Types of Budget

A budget may be of an *Envelope* category if all your income is divided into envelopes based on identified items/activities. Should the money allocated for an item get exhausted, there is no further expenditure on the same item except money is taken from another envelop. This is good for people who want to stay out of debt.

The *50-30-20* budget is for those aspiring for the achievement of some financial goals. The philosophy is about allocating 50% of income for needs, 30% for wants and 20% for savings and debt repayments.

The *zero-based budget* indicates that your account will have a zero balance within the budget period. It makes you spend to the last currency on identified activities. It is to achieve maximum use of the money making sure every unit of the currency counts. It is good for those who want to keep track and monitor their expenditure pattern.

The *5 Category budget* is about determining five basic needs and assigning expenditure portfolio to each. The needs may be rent, healthcare, utilities, entertainment and car maintenance.

Guidelines in Making a Personal Budget

1. Gather information on all your financial statements.
2. Add up all your inflows. In a case that it varies, use the lowest within the past year as the baseline figure.
3. List your monthly expenses, dividing them into mandatory and discretionary expenses. The mandatory expenses include rent, electricity, food, healthcare, and the like. The discretionary list includes Television subscription, clothing, travel, and house cleaning, among others.
4. Assign spending limits to the expenses within your income.
5. Subtract expenses from total income. If your income is more than the expenses, you may adopt the 50-30-20 budgeting philosophy.
6. Review and adjust expenses accordingly. The expenses worksheet shown below may guide further. It helps estimate your monthly expenses. The sum total of the expenses is deducted from the total monthly income and thereafter adjusted in line with your budget. Carefully followed, you can stay within your means and reduce expenditure stress. It is important to remind that all expenditure should focus on quality of life rather than just saving money.

Expense Category	Monthly Amount
Housing	
Mortgage/Rent	₦
Property taxes	₦
Rent	₦
Utilities	₦
Maintenance/fees	₦
Food	
Groceries	₦
Self appreciation	₦
Transportation	
Vehicle maintenance	₦
Fuel	₦
Auto insurance	₦
Public transportation	₦
Health care	
Medical services	₦
Medications and supplies	₦
Health insurance	₦
Personal insurance	
Life insurance	₦
Disability insurance	₦
Personal care	
Clothing	₦
Products and services	₦

Family care	
Children/Spouse	₦
Miscellaneous	
Loans	₦
Entertainment	₦
Travel/Vacation	₦
Hobbies	₦
Gifts/Donations	₦
Education	₦
Others	₦
Total monthly expenses	

Fig. 3: Retirement Expenses Worksheet

CHAPTER ELEVEN

PERSONAL LIFE STORIES FROM THE HEART

When we least expect it, life sets us a challenge to test our courage and willingness to change: at such a moment, there is no point in pretending that nothing has happened or in saying that we are yet ready. The challenge will not wait. Life does not look back. Paulo Coelho

Some of these stories may assist in achieving a meaningful retirement. What early cohorts did, how they did and when they did it can help in changing the retirement narrative for new or intending retirees. Personal stories help in influencing ideas and opinions.

1. The Bicycle-riding retired Permanent Secretary that sits on the board of Educational Institutions (Elder Ubong R. Akpan)

My Experience in Retirement

I served in the public service of my state notionally for thirty-five years, in real terms for thirty-four years. What difference does that make anyway? A lot! As a spiritual principle, the heavens bare rule. A man's mind will govern the direction and state of his body, even as a man's psychological state, conditions the state of his body. To have to disengage one year short of expected period can and does make, often a vast difference in post service life and experience. The psychology of it, is vastly significant.

Preparation for Retirement

Fourteen years into my service, I was moved from being a field officer, a classroom teacher to serving as a Pension schedule officer. The significance of that move was beyond varied experience but in exposure to certain skills, competencies and knowledge, that placed me in a position to be of help to myself, friends and associates who needed to prepare for retirement. Preparation needs to be in two major areas: finance and psychological adjustment. I knew and taught in many Workshops and Seminars as Resource Person and Facilitator, that you need to save and invest and that you need to psychologically prepare for post service life.

Nothing like the Experience

No matter what you know, nothing quite prepares you for the real experience. I taught people to save, but did not quite save enough myself. The reality of life in a developing economy is that wages are inadequate to pay your bills. As the parlance here goes, 'your take home pay cannot take you home'. Nevertheless, those in long-term paid employment and indeed all must cultivate the habit of saving and investing during active service period. Financial education right from basic education level should be helpful here.

Adjustment and Mal-Adjustment

One has to prepare to adjust to the new pattern of existence. I never woke up to prepare for the office as some of my colleagues did. I did not have to face the embarrassment of arriving in the office to find another on my table, but I lost my time management skills, especially waking in the morning with time on my hands and nothing to do and no plans for the day. The implication of that is late mornings and early breakfasts. The worst is the effect of inactivity on health, fortunately for me, I have always lived a very active life. I exercise, I have four bicycles in my stable, I ride round the compound, do twelve kilometres to a nearby local government area every Saturday. Ride to visit friends around and sit down to some conversations.

Part of the mal-adjustment I see all around is the unwillingness to accept that we need rest after a certain period and age. Colleagues are going into more stressful businesses, opening schools and are directly involved in the management, commercial activities that necessitate long hours of sitting in fixed positions, opening churches, running ministries, establishing manufacturing and production concerns without adequate preparations with heavy tolls on their health.

I have found more time now for a greater involvement in community development activities. My skills, competencies and experience in government and as a licensed HR practitioner has stood me in good stead for light business engagements, consulting for schools in the areas of recruitment and learning/ development programmes. I sit on the Board of various educational institutions. However, the disadvantage is that many want to take advantage of my passion for value addition to obtain my service without adequate reward and compensation.

I also have enough time for leisure. I used to read voraciously, I enjoy travels but both have been hampered by two aspects of current experience that should receive our next attention and these are lethargy and poor finances. Lethargy is an experience I find very debilitating. I experience a slower response to planned activities. I find it difficult to meet my schedule in reading and writing. I take very long time to initiate action on requests made on me to write proposals, memos, develop administrative instruments and templates. Once however, I am able to break to a start, I do not have any problem going through with it. Similarly, I find strength for sustained reading waning. I spend longer time on each volume and meeting the yearly target of fifty- two volumes is becoming difficult to achieve.

Finance

The current template for a seamless transfer from the salary to pension platform of payment is to be commended. I therefore did not experience any undue financial stress after retirement. Although it is possible to move from one platform to the other if we begin to process for retirement early enough, I did not have that experience. I disengaged in August and payment of my pension commenced in December. This was on account of the fact that I did not begin processing ahead of time. Once I started, however, the process was smooth.

In the period of three months when I neither received salary nor pension, I was sustained by proceeds of Life Assurance, a five-year Savings/ Investment which was part of my preparation for retirement. I am currently on another more ambitious Life Assurance Savings/ Investment plan which is proving to be very challenging. My finance definitely would have been healthier and my retirement experience more pleasant and beneficial, if my gratuity had been received.

Health

By the grace of God, I have always enjoyed sound health with rarely any crisis. I suffer none of the debilitating conditions that constitute a drain on resources. I certainly have enough time now for leisure, less stress, more exercises, routine wellness procedure; warm water and lemon every morning, more of vegies and herbs rather than synthetic drugs which in any case is rarely necessary. Once, however, I experienced a condition associated with aging, prostrate being a threat. After three weeks with sour-sop leaves, the entire thing was blasted. I wholly believe that health is a product of lifestyle, and that understanding is guiding my attitude to life. It is beneficial and to be highly recommended.

Concluding Remarks

I believe we need to be honest with ourselves about life and be properly guided by that value in all we do. We need to serve honestly and passionately, love passionately, give freely and live for more than ourselves and interest. We need to rest; we cannot work for ever. God made provision for rest and provided for a Sabbath rest for man and the entire creation, once every week, seven years and after forty-nine years, a greater Sabbath called JUBILEE. We should fully enjoy our leisure, relax, laugh at life and not take ourselves too seriously. We should make friends freely but keep the good ones. This life is all about relationships, we should learn to be good at managing and sustaining relationships.

Most importantly, we were created worship beings, that is purpose, divine purpose. We must love God passionately and follow his purpose on this side of eternity.*"He has showed you, O man, what is good. And what does the LORD require of you? To act justly and to love mercy and to walk humbly with your God" (Micah 6:8 NIV)* It pays at this period to begin to pursue higher values and deeper meaning to life, and to seek things of more beneficial permanence.

2. This 105-Year-Old Martini Lover Has Been Retired for Almost 40 Years. Here Are Her Smartest Money Moves[8]

Start Saving Early

Harrington started socking away quarters as a girl of about 13, storing each one she found in a vase. Today, some people do the same with each $5 bill they come across, and the amounts are roughly equivalent: back in 1931, when Harrington started her habit, a quarter was worth just under $5.

She continued saving quarters into adulthood, and she says the money became her travel fund. She taught and supervised teachers in the Boston public schools until retiring at age 67 and took her trips during school vacations. Favorite European destinations included Malta, Italy, France and England. "I loved it all over there," she says.

Harrington married for the first time at 67, wedding a college beau who had been widowed. Her husband died about six years later, and Harrington moved in with her nephew, George Lyons, his wife, Ann, and their three young daughters. Harrington used $100,000 from her savings to contribute to the down payment on the house Lyons purchased for everyone to share.

Lyons worked with a lawyer to protect his aunt's investment in the house he bought. He'd heard of cases where a co-living arrangement went sour, and he drew up a contract so that Harrington didn't lose her investment if they decided to part ways. "As much as we loved each other dearly, it doesn't always work out," Lyons says.

But it did work out, and the extended family remains happily together 30 years later. "I love the set up," Harrington says.

Secure Guaranteed Income

Harrington has multiple guaranteed income sources to support her longevity. She has a pension from the Boston school system and about $1,700 in Social Security that she collects on her late husband's record. Even though she had her own career, she wasn't eligible for Social Security: certain state and local government employees don't pay Social Security payroll taxes and thus can't collect benefits.

Harrington also has an annuity she recalls buying from a salesman her school headmaster invited to speak to teachers when she was in her late 50s or early 60s. "I decided to buy one then and there," she says.

It was a good move. The deferred annuity started paying Harrington about $195 a month when she was in her 70s. This modest amount has added up over the decades: Lyons estimates that so far his aunt has collected tens of thousands of dollars more than she put into the annuity. Insurance companies can't have too many customers who live well into their 100s, or they'd go out of business. "They've lost money big time on her," Lyons says.

Nurture Your Passion

Harrington got her first music education as a child from the nuns of Notre Dame in the Roxbury neighborhood of Boston. "They were wonderful teachers," she says.

She followed their footsteps and began teaching music herself. "I loved the children and I loved the music," she says.

Harrington volunteered giving tours of Boston Symphony Hall until she was 85. These days, she can no longer see well, but Harrington can still listen to Mozart, Haydn and other favorite composers. She has a Google Home device and enjoys directing it to "play Frank Sinatra."

She participates in the New England Centenarian Study at Boston Medical Center and plans to donate her brain to Alzheimer's research. "It's not because I think I'm so smart," Harrington is quick to say. But she does believe her adaptability has helped her stay sharp at such an advanced age: "I can make changes and not be unhappy."

3. Patrick T. Edem, the retired Federal Quantity Surveyor that preaches Christ

I joined the Federal Civil Service as a Quantity Surveyor, Grade 2 in 1987 and was posted to the Federal Ministry of Works and Housing on a starting basic salary of N324.50. This pay was the prevailing salary of a graduate officer within my rank approved by government since the late nineteen seventies. At the time of this salary approval, the exchange rate between United State Dollar and Naira was about 60 Cents to one Naira. This translated in value to $540 USD. In 2020, the same employee as a Deputy Director on Grade Level 16 Step 9 earns on the average N193,000 or $440 USD with an expected monthly pension of N70,000 or $150USD after 35 years of meritorious service. What a shame? What could this amount actually purchase at the present cost of living in Nigeria? Most of us have retired into poverty except those who were 'smart' and exploited the system. It is appalling to note that nearly one year after my retirement from the Federal Civil Service as a Deputy Director, I do not have an idea of what my benefits will amount to in real and concrete terms and when it will eventually be paid. Situations like this have further identified my country, Nigeria as the poorest in the world, despite her wealth of resources.

Preparation

Retirement is an event with a date in mind and this is why preparation should be properly situated. To me, retirement does not necessarily mean cessation from work but a change in work assignments and working schedule. It is only important that every individual approaching retirement should have made up his or her mind on what kind of work is suitable and available for this period of one's life time in order to achieve a meaningful retirement.

As a professional Quantity Surveyor with over thirty years of post-qualification cognate experience, the first thing that came to mind was professional practice. This was adequately thought about with a registered firm in place. However, this would not work for me because I do have other ideas coupled with competing social demands and commitments already in place. Social demands and commitments prompted me to engage myself in public speaking, book writing, internet business and foreign exchange trading trainings during the last one year in my paid employment.

My first line of interest and also within my competence is pastoral ministry in the Christian faith as a gospel ambassador. To this end, I was ordained minister of the gospel. My area of interest is in doctrinal development and edification through training. The ministry runs a-one-month intensive training for ministers.

Before now, my one-year pre-retirement was loaded because I got engaged in book writing clinics and training in order to enhance my teaching and writing ability. This I did with a prolific writer, coach and trainer who set up his outfit after years as a bank employee.

From a personal experience, no retiree should engage in any work or business he or she does not have some element of competency in and would be able to supervise personally. Four years before my retirement, I had set up a bakery and confectionaries business in Abuja. My inexperience in the area led me to lose my entire savings.

Conclusion

I may not be wealthy but I am confident in the good health which to me, is the greatest asset. I have peace, relate well with my family and always in tune with my maker. To the un-initiated, make plans and 'dig your well before you drink'

4. Stumbling Towards Retirement[9]

The last thing I expected at age 50, after 30 years of full-time employment, was to find myself preparing to attend tractor trailer school. It was a surprising journey. I was a partner at a large private equity firm. I really enjoyed my work and my colleagues. Why was I feeling increasingly unsettled? I finally came to terms with the fact that I wanted to start a new phase of life, so I made the difficult decision to retire.

My hope was that I could put my technical experience to use helping others. I envisioned that retirement meant no longer ceding control of my time and personal priorities to the inevitable demands of a full-time job. At the same time, I was scared by such a radical change with so little certainty about the outcome. My greatest fear was that I would become irrelevant. At the request of my partners, I deferred acting on my decision for a year. I was secretly relieved when they delayed me from actually taking the leap.

During that time I spoke to a number of friends, acquaintances, and strangers who retired after long and successful careers. I figured I could learn much from their experiences to help me prepare for my own transition. I was surprised and disheartened by what I discovered. Little did I know that they would add to my trepidation as I struggled to put every piece in place before leaving my job. The pieces weren't connecting and too many seemed to be missing. It felt like I was preparing for a trip and couldn't figure out what to pack. It took me too long to realize that retirement entailed embarking with empty luggage and figuring out what to pack along the way.

Some people I spoke to were at peace with their decision, but a disheartening number of retired professionals were adrift and unhappy. They craved the fulfillment, recognition, and rewards enjoyed during active employment. They added to my own fears because I did not expect to find them so desperately trying to recreate the same external structure during retirement. Most disturbingly, many admitted to being lonely as they gradually lost the cohort that anchored them during their working career.

While many people retire by choice, an increasing number of productive professionals are forced to retire prematurely because of ageism, buyouts or layoffs. Even though I retired under different circumstances, I am acutely sensitive to the pain, frustration and financial hardship that can accompany such a brutal and unwanted transition. I have also been humbled by the experience of those who chose retirement to take on the role of primary caregiver for aging parents. That is such a challenging circumstance that I do not feel I have standing to offer any observations, just deep respect.

A friend recently asked me how I shaped my retirement in light of the many retired professionals he knows who are unmoored. To paraphrase him, "They were at the top of their game and now they are confused and cannot figure out what to do with their lives. They feel like no one returns their calls". My friend was intrigued by my own stumbles and subsequent discoveries over the past decade. He suggested I write up an account of my experience so others might find it easier to chart a course that can work for them.

Looking back over the past 10 years, I now realize that my own mis-steps paved the way for a more enjoyable and balanced future. Those often harsh lessons informed a framework that evolved to start working for me. The frustrations of the first few years "out of work" eventually gave way to a more fun and interesting phase of life. With that in mind, I hope that you might benefit from what I learned during the twisting journey from employment to retirement.

Of course, anyone contemplating retirement will have to frame an approach that works for them. For what it is worth, here is mine.

Constructing an internal resume

Many people who have enjoyed a successful career have been rewarded with relevance. Unfortunately, some have not. Relevance comes in many forms: public accolades, respect from colleagues, deep and unique expertise, financial success, assistance to others, a fancy office, a beautiful home. You get the idea.

Some of these accomplishments are universally lauded and admired. Others are usually deemed to be superficial and self-indulgent. Regardless, they all shape our own perception of personal relevance. I'm sure you know countless "successful" people who try to impress by convincing themselves that what they can buy and what they can control makes them relevant. I learned the hard way that relevance purchased is not relevance earned.

When I was struggling with "how to retire", the most impactful insight came from Tom Gilovich, a leading psychologist and former chair of the Cornell Psychology Department. He told me that I was more likely to find fulfillment and balance in retirement if I focused on my "internal resume" and stopped worrying about my external resume. He observed that many successful people have dense external resumes and surprisingly sparse internal resumes.

Our external resumes are chock full of degrees, accomplishments, and other validating signals of success. I assume many of you are justifiably proud of your external resume. At the same time, our external resumes rarely reveal much about our values, passions, commitments outside of work or the relationships that matter most to us. That's where the internal resume comes into play. Our internal resumes are focused on personal values and the focus we bring to activities that exclusively nurture our inner sense of purpose, or the impact we have on others. Most importantly, no one else will see your internal resume. You only write it for yourself and you are the only person who edits it.

I often reflect on Tom's observations because they stood out then and still do today. As a result, I reframed my approach to retirement.

Instead of prioritizing activities and relationships that were vital during my working career, I now find myself focusing on developing new relationships, new skills to serve others and maximizing autonomy from unwanted obligations.

Even though I am often asked to describe my internal resume in detail, that's not how it works. Suffice it to say that a few concrete examples are the best I can offer. I started teaching, asked three coaches to help guide me in learning new skills, fulfilled a long held dream to go to tractor-trailer school, lent my technical skills to some national security challenges, and sought out non-profit entrepreneurs who are gearing-up to tackle unmet needs. It might take longer than you are comfortable with to refine your priorities to the point where you no longer feel like you are grasping to find purpose. It's worth the wait...

You'll be surprised how many apparently relevant activities suggested by others don't deserve an entry on your internal resume. You'll be liberated when you say "no" to suggestions that you might have jumped at in the past because they enhanced your external resume. The shift from "yes" to "no" will liberate you as it starts to feel comfortable and justified. It didn't exactly start off that way...

The perils of over-commitment

I was scared by the disturbing conversations I had with those who were adrift. I was scared that my phone would stop ringing. I was scared that my hard-earned professional expertise would be deemed obsolete. I was scared that I would not be invited to engage in professional activities. I was scared that I would become irrelevant as my external resume stagnated. I was scared to retire.

Because of this self-perceived void, I committed too early and too often to activities that, in hindsight, were unjustified. Looking from the outside, you probably would have endorsed most of my choices. Looking from the inside, I was increasingly unhappy with the prospect of what retirement was offering. My wife was also critical of my choices. My misallocation of time was a painful stumble. The worst part is that my most valued mentors (you know who you are) strongly advised me against over-commitment during my initial transition. I ignored their advice and paid the price for doing so. You've been warned. If you choose to make the same mistake, don't blame me.

It took me several years to unwind those premature decisions and ill-advised commitments. I regret the wasted time, dissipated resources, and strained relationships. I strongly recommend you not commit to anything until you are sure that it deserves a place on your internal resume. Three months of recognizing my fear for what it was, and sidelining myself to reflect on how to reframe relevance, would have saved a lot of frustration and regret.

Time is NOT money

I got lucky in my professional career. Undoubtedly many of you did too. As a result, you may have freedom to spend time on activities that are not necessarily focused on personal earnings or profit. I am especially mindful that many people still need to generate income in retirement. I hope my experience is helpful, regardless of individual economic circumstances.

You won't be surprised to learn that when you value your time at $0/hour, there will be unlimited demand to consume it. Most of my early commitments were made as a "favor" to someone to whom I felt obligated. A few of these activities were fulfilling. Most were not. All took more of my time than I expected…and too much time to conclude or unwind.

I hope you are wiser than I was and do not over-commit, but that's only half the battle. Any time devoted to others, whether it is compensated or not, has to earn a place on your internal resume. If you don't want it there...then you'll be much better off by saying no.

But as usual, it's never that easy. We all have obligations that can't be ignored, regardless of whether we are retired or not. What's less obvious is how people, including people you really care about, will react when you say no to their request for a commitment of your time. I'm still taken aback by some of the responses I get when I say no to requests for "a short meeting", "a quick phone call", "an urgent email", "a chance to mentor a promising young professional", "the opportunity to engage with a deserving non-profit" or "a compelling investment opportunity".

Suffice it to say that "no" does not bring out the best in people. If it sounds selfish, that's only because I spent too much time responding affirmatively to other people's priorities. My poor triage for the first few years after retiring was a waste on many levels. The converse is so much better. When you do say yes, it will be with genuine commitment and a sense of deep satisfaction when your impact is positive and meaningful. Empty time is a privilege and a reservoir of power and potential that you should not squander. You'll fill it when the time is right, and feel good about it when you do.

When you come to a fork in the road...take it!

Some people retire to bring renewed focus to a primary activity or passion that is important to them. I completely understand and celebrate that choice. I eventually came to understand that I needed to travel a different path.

My priorities are to get on the steepest learning curve possible, to avoid interactions with toxic people and to refocus on individuals rather than on institutions. This led me to construct a "portfolio" of loosely related activities in four areas that are relevant to me. These are entirely personal choices that I could not choose in the prior 30 years of working for an employer. My approach is no better or worse than the alternative of a more unified focus. All I know is that regardless of which fork you choose on the path to retirement, there is one path that is almost certainly going to end in tears.

Past has to be context for our future, but you'll likely join the ranks of the unmoored if you strive to recreate your professional past in retirement. Many struggling professionals think that they'll regain their sense of purpose and externally validating structure by joining boards, focusing on non-profit activities, and investing in small companies to counsel entrepreneurs. All of these activities can be fun and fulfilling, but not if they are an attempt to continue filling in your external resume.

I learned the hard way that public boards can be a major hassle and create too much stress for too little return. Hopefully you'll find more fulfillment on that audit committee than I did. Many non-profits are looking only for a checkbook and have little interest in operational engagement from board members/donors. And sadly, many young entrepreneurs are not really interested in advice from a well meaning, retired expert who wants to "coach" them.

At the risk of sounding overly prescriptive, file your external resume away with all those lucite tombstones that no one cares about but you and your cleaning person. Only you can definitively decide if you want to create a new portfolio of activities or primarily focus on a personal passion. Either path can be more balanced and satisfying than you expect…and might unnecessarily fear.

We're in this together

Although it might seem obvious, retirement really does require a challenging re-definition of your relationship with your spouse/

partner/significant other. We've all heard funny stories of the retiree who re-organizes the spice drawer. I was much more enlightened...I reorganized the book shelf on my first day of retirement (no joke).

Seriously though, because I over-committed so early I did not leave room for the inevitable partnership rebalancing that must come when you retire. I'm lucky that my wife, who was already retired, called me out and insisted that I stop trying to recreate my past. She's the one who recognized my unjustified fear of irrelevance for what it was. She kept insisting I would still be relevant in a different way. I refused to believe her. She was right. I was wrong. Who knew marriage could be so complicated?

If you allow for it, you'll eventually find a new steady state that leaves room to spend time together in ways that were not possible when working full-time. Of course, synchronizing with a working partner poses a whole other set of issues I'm not qualified to address. Fortunately, my wife and I finally figured out what works for us, but I have to admit that she has no interest in spending all her time with me. Who can blame her?

The biggest surprise

I spent the first stage of retirement trawling my contacts for lunch dates, coffee and other activities with people I knew. It filled my time. It was sometimes interesting. It was no different than when I was working. I already knew these people and felt a little desperate trying to catch-up on professional lives and situations I had formerly been part of. I was taking a misguided approach to stave off the loneliness that afflicts so many middle-aged retirees. I came to realize that, along with focus on my internal resume, I needed to find a new cohort populated by people I did not already know. I gave priority to those who were doing things that had nothing to do with my prior career. As I write this, I am smiling because I just got an email from an expert woodworker who has become a friend. We never would have met if I didn't spot his work and make the effort to seek him out. I can count many other interactions like this. I've serendipitously met soldiers, academics, magicians, physicians, poker players, entrepreneurs, and especially truck driving instructors, who have enriched my life since I stopped working. Many of these people don't share much in common with my former colleagues, but they sure are fun, often humbling, and personally enriching to hang out with. I know you are never supposed to eat lunch alone, but it gets even better when you eat lunch with someone you don't know. It takes work and some chutzpah, but you'll have more time to get used to it when you retire.

The Bottom Line

Every retirement looks different and what works for me may not even be close to what works for you. I do know for sure that you will be stuck in a holding pattern if you wait until every piece is lined up before taking the plunge. Don't worry about packing your bags. You'll be off to a good start if you focus on enhancing your internal resume, protecting empty time, redefining your relationship with your life partner, engaging with a new cohort, and choosing a primary focus or a portfolio of activities. You'll discover that you're relevant in new and surprising ways. Your calls will be returned. You'll learn a lot about life that you don't already know and, if you really want to have some fun, you can always learn how to parallel park a 70 foot tractor trailer.

Good luck writing your next chapter. I hope we get to share discoveries over lunch.

5. Lady Elizabeth Joseph Ogah, a Retired Nurse-turned Baker in retirement counsels on Retirement Plan from First Day of Appointment

The statutory retirement age in my State Civil Service is 60 years of age or 35 years of active service, whichever comes first. After retirement, civil servants are entitled to benefits such as gratuity and monthly pensions.

I retired from the Service last year, April, 2019. At retirement, I was 53 years of age and had clocked the statutory 35 years of active service. I had worked as a nurse. Retirement, I must say is another phase of life which if not properly planned for can be very disastrous. It is a "must come" for every worker. Therefore, preparing for retirement is key to a successful retirement life.

The office I occupied before retirement actually helped me to have insight into how to prepare for my exit from service. I was privileged to be trained few years before I finally retired. With this, I was equipped and thereafter ventured into bread baking (production) and fish farming.

After retirement, I still wake up early to check on my business. This has kept me very active as I used to be when I was a civil servant, though not under compulsion. There is liberty to either leave early or later. It has been a very good transitory period for me.

However, my pension was not paid immediately after retirement. It took three (3) good months before Government started paying my pension. Truly, my business sustained me and cushioned the effect of non-payment of pension. I still have good reasons to be happy and thankful because before this present Government came on board, retirees were paid after one (1) year though with their gratuity. What is obtainable now is that you get your pension paid without gratuity.

The last paid gratuity was to those who retired in 2015. They have just started paying January and February 2016's list in 2020.

Government should be sensitive enough to the plight of the retirees by paying up their benefits as and when due. This would go a long way in alleviating unnecessary suffering for those who have worked for Government throughout their active years.

Nevertheless, for me, retirement is a blessing in disguise. I now have quality time with my family; we pray together and become more united in God's presence. I have been able to adopt a healthy lifestyle exercising in the morning and eating healthy foods, no more junk. Retirement has actually helped me to rediscover myself. I am in a better position to advise civil servants to plan well for retirement, which I have been doing passionately.

In conclusion, I want to say as you get your first Appointment letter into employment, start planning for retirement as the key to a beautiful and successful life thereafter.

6. 'How I built my retirement investment'

In Summary:

> Hosea Kili, the managing director of CPF Trust Fund Group adds that upon retirement, expenses usually reduce by 30 per cent but the retiree has to figure out how to cater for 70 percent of their monthly expenses.

The Kimuyus constructed a hotel that does not serve alcohol. A lush green façade adorns Convent International Hotel in Nairobi's Lavington, built by Abednego Kimuyu and his wife Alice. The two are pastors and their hotel does not serve alcohol.

For the Kimuyus, the hotel is an early retirement investment that they envisioned when they were still employed. Abednego worked as a banker for 28 years before he took an early retirement in 2011 to concentrate on his business while Alice kept her job at the Ministry of Agriculture before following suit.

"Once you are hired, know that one day you will leave that employment to concentrate on what you love most or confront misery in its true form — poverty in your twilight years. It is up to you to decide early what you want to become or how you will spend your 'free' time," says Abednego.

He adds that retirement is never a surprise but an eventuality that should enable one to utilise experience learnt during their working life, savings made, and realise the dream of re-inventing themselves.

"It must be a time to enjoy and must never be a struggle," he says.

"Work to invest, gain experience and get exposure for better networks as well as raise capital via savings. Spend all your employment years identifying your next business after retirement," says Alice who is 61 years old.

Abednego bought a half acre plot in Lavington where he planned to build a home but changed his mind in 2009 and constructed a one-storeyed hotel with 10 rooms.

"It was soon overwhelmed by client demand and we took a loan that we added with part of our savings to expand the hotel. We now have five conference rooms, a restaurant, an open garden party area as well as an executive boardroom," he says.

Succession

Abednego studied Mathematics and Computer Science and later pursued a master's degree in Business Administration majoring in entrepreneurship at Massachusetts University in the United States.

He worked at KCB Group for 28 years in various sections, including general operations, mortgage financing and credit risk management.

"Despite the years of expertise in the financial sector, I could not start a bank because it requires a lot of capital. I wanted to build an enterprise that revolves around people. I opted for a hotel that rides on Christian values which gives me an avenue to continue serving people" says the father of three. For a retirement investment to pay off, Abednego says, it has to be professionally run.

"We have retained architects and a landscape architect as well as tree and flower nursery operator. This ensures everything is planned for. Any expansion is informed by demand. Do not get into a business just because your friend has succeeded. Study and venture on your personal path," he adds.

With clear structures that enable the hotel to run even without their close supervision, the Kimuyus can easily engage in their passions like travelling and attending church meetings across the world.

"Our children are not in the business. Their role is first to pursue their education and later join in. The experience they gain out there is crucial to take this business to the next level. One works in a bank in Australia, another works as a finance officer in a non-governmental organization while our last born just graduated as a lawyer," Abednego says.

"Allowing children into a business quickly portends a disaster since they have no work ethics but raw power and access to finances. Wielding enormous power erodes the corporate culture needed to drive a business to another level," he adds.

Married for 36 years, the couple says their sojourn in Nairobi will be short-lived as they are currently concentrating on a farm that also supplies fresh foodstuff to their hotel.

"Old people have no place in a fast lane Nairobi. Will motorists tolerate an old man who slowly crosses the road? As one gets older, you need to return home where you will enjoy utmost respect among your community as an opinion leader," he says.

Early investment

Retirement is a puzzle that many Kenyans struggle to solve. According to Octagon Africa Financial Services, the lowest one should save for retirement is KSh100(Sh3,400) a day or between KSh3,000 (about Sh103,000) to KSh4,000 a month which will give one up to KSh3 million(about Sh34m) in pension savings upon attainment of 60 years.

Avoid instant gratification in favour of a pension plan that will offer long-term gain, says Fred Waswa, the Octagon Africa chief executive.

"If you want to enjoy your free time travelling the world to see wildlife, swim in oceans and attend global or regional cultural activities annually, then set aside an extra KSh100(Sh3,400) a day or KSh3,000 (about Sh103,000) a month for that purpose. Set aside more money for the fun things you plan to do upon retirement as the pension's kitty should remain intact for one purpose — sustaining your livelihood," he says.

Hosea Kili, the managing director of CPF Trust Fund Group adds that upon retirement, expenses usually reduce by 30 per cent but the retiree has to figure out how to cater for 70 percent of their monthly expenses.

"Savings for retirement will then come in handy. Each individual's expenses are different and this should inform the savings' plan one should have," he says.

But Hosea advises retirees not to venture into investments that they are not very conversant with. Remember, the essence is to have a relatively hassle-free business that will finance your sunset years and hobbies.

Trick

Avoid instant gratification in favor of a pension's plan that will offer long-term gain.

By James Kariuki of *Daily Mirror August 23,2020*

CHAPTER TWELVE

FINISHING MEANINGFULLY STRONG

> *...believe that your greatest contribution is always ahead of you. You might retire from a job, but never retire from making contribution, not accumulation.* Hyrum W. Smith

Terry Fox, a Canadian athlete was diagnosed with bone cancer at 18 years of age which caused his right leg to be amputated. He had two choices: remain in the hospital and die or find meaning in life. He opted for the second. For the purpose of raising one million dollars for cancer research, he set a goal of running across Canada with his one natural leg to inspire millions of people to donate towards that purpose. He died before he could finish his Marathon of Hope race but, successfully raised 24.6 million dollars. This effort brought him to limelight and created a worldwide legacy of an annual Terry Fox race which so far has raised over 750 million dollars for cancer research purpose.

The above story buttresses the fact that there can be a fortune in an unfortunate situation or circumstance, if only we consider such an opportunity worth exploiting. At the verge of death, Terry was still hopeful with plans for the future. He became a global celebrity. If he could defy a dreadful and terminal health condition like cancer, then the challenges of retirement can be tamed, subdued and overpowered.

So what is your attitude towards retirement? A positive disposition ennobles a meaningful retirement through the generation of a positive magnetic field. Positive thoughts calm emotions and create an environment that radiates life and a future. Are your thoughts positive? Signs are you won't fear any change, you will be willing to learn from your mistakes, you will feel grateful for what you have, you will accept others' differences gracefully, you will trust your judgement, and you will set goals and persevere to achieve them, just as you will take responsibility for your actions.

No matter how others fare in retirement, you can make the difference. There are people that have been successful in braking long-held assumptions in many fields, some at the risk of their lives. Retirement is too small to intimidate you. Chuck Yeager, for instance proved a scientific assumption wrong in 1947 by becoming the first pilot to have exceeded the speed of sound in aviation flight. Before then, it was believed the plane would burn at that speed. Christopher Columbus proved the earth was spherical in shape, against the thoughts of his time. An Italian inventor, Alessandro Volta in 1800, proved to his world he was not a heretic after all by inventing the electric bulb that 'shone like the sun'. Before then, he was seen as attempting to equate himself with God with his electric bulb-making idea. Again, until recently peptic ulcer was assumed to have been caused by excess stomach acid as against the proven bacterial infection called *helicobacter pylori.* The acids were symptoms but doctors continued regarding them as the cause.

Whatever experience or assumption others may have had may not apply to you if you positively apply yourself to retirement. The mind has a power of its own. Once an idea is conceived, it can be given birth to. Concerning the mind, Confucius reiterated 'the General of a large army may be defeated, but you cannot defeat the determined mind of a peasant'. Meaningful retirement does not evolve on its own. It starts from the mind, so activate your mind. Do not be too rational. Do not be linear in thinking. Do not surround your thoughts around the present. Do not use money as the measurement for everything. Do not expect an avocation to turn into a vocation on its own. Challenge widely held assumptions. Just hope to make a difference.

At 94, Pa Reuben Fasoranti was still teaching and meeting with his teachers. In an interview in *Punch* newspaper of September 25, 2020, he said 'After retirement, I went back to teaching. I founded Omolere Nursery and Primary School and after that, I founded the Akure High School, which is still there till today….It has been a lovely time for me'. He had decided to make a difference and therefore planned ahead.

Having a meaningful retirement requires a plan. There is this popular aphorism that '*he who fails to plan, plans to fail*'. Planning is the process of establishing a future course of action with the expectation of a beneficial outcome. A plan must recognise current realities. They come in dimensions of short-term (within 6 months), medium-term (within 18 months) and long-term (over 18 months). A good plan must have goals, purpose, mission and vision.

A goal is the target which provides excellent opportunities to build your confidence. Goals are futuristic and must be written, committed to, shared and open to constant evaluation.

Purpose on the other hand is what you want your life to represent. It is the reason for Living. It can be almost anything but, it has to be there. Michel de Montaigne is of the opinion that 'the great and glorious masterpiece of man is to know how to live to purpose'. It is the essence of life. For a retiree, it is a meaningful retirement.

The process of establishing a purpose requires self-reflection and pondering on the injustices that bother you, interaction with others as well as passionate things of your life. Your purpose must be visionary and worthwhile. You need to ask such questions like: will I live a meaningful life in retirement? What should I do to lead a meaningful retirement life? What will I want my life to stand for? What important contribution(s) will I make in retirement? These and similar other questions must align with your natural talents, values, passion and mission. Do not imitate others as people are wont to. In the words of Eric Hoffer 'when people are free to do as they please, they usually imitate each other'. You may adapt but, try as much as you can to be yourself in your new found freedom.

Mission answers to what you are or will be doing as a retiree. There must be a specific and definite engagement. The supreme value is not the future but, the present. It may be community service, book writing, farming or whatever. But, resting cannot be an engagement. Idling away is not a mission. So what is your mission?

And, as the saying goes *people without vision perish.* Vision is the desired and expected outcome. Vision is seeing beyond the horizon, a perception of future reality and a higher state of consciousness. So, you need a carefully designed plan for your retirement. This may be built on the following:

1. Health

   Health plays a prominent role in meaningful retirement and there is a huge cost associated with elderly healthcare. A study indicated that an average of $18,424 was spent on persons of 65 years and above between 1996 and 2010. This figure will certainly be higher as the years go by hence, healthcare plans should incorporate health insurance options if available in your environment. Regular medical checks should be a practice. Remember, 'prevention is better than cure'

On health, Dr. David Sinclair, an acclaimed Harvard Medical School scientist noted that 'intermittent fasting, cold exposure, exercising with the right intensity and eating less meat have been shown to help us live younger and healthier for longer'. Scientists at UC Irvine, a public research university added that smoking is dangerous, daily exercise is important; social interaction with friends is needed; moderate alcohol is fine, a cup of coffee per day would not hurt; vitamins do not make a difference and an average weight is good.

The importance of the mind in health issues has been emphasised. The *Journal of American Medical Association,* opines that those already with health setback have 44% recovery rate if they adopt a positive outlook. Spending time with little ones you love is known to impact positively on and radiate health. It is also advisable to sit less as longer sitting time has been linked to increased death from cardiovascular diseases and cancer.

2. Finance

The *Northwestern Mutual Survey* Report indicated that finances are the main source of stress among Americans. While money and financial security remain important, they do not guarantee any peace of mind. When we were young, we believed money could do everything but, as we grew older we realise that it is what we do with money that can give us happiness. The import of this statement comes with the experience of a former school mate. In the 1990s, he was a topflight banker and making waves in the industry. He was young, had the needed professional papers and his career progression was meteoric. He lived in an expansive mansion in an exclusive part of the Central city. The family was fine, they could travel overseas for holidays; could donate a 48-seater Toyota Coaster bus for a good cause and the children attended expensive schools.

But, this is the same person that subsequently told me in a personal conversation that 'there are things money cannot buy'. I had heard that statement before but, it was from thence it made a great meaning to me. For a meaningful life in retirement, money is important, but peace of mind is more important.

And, let me digress a little. Which money personality class do you belong? Understanding your money personality will assist your financial plan as your genes, habits and attitudes determine your peculiar personality. The knowledge will enhance money management skills. People read books, attend Seminars and even pray to God on ways of making money, but hardly do they enquire on how to spend the money they have. Money personalities are as follows:

People of the *Big spenders'* category are those that are never afraid to spend. The ease of spending may have a motivation in the success in acquiring basic needs hence not afraid of poverty. If you belong to this category, the disadvantage is that much spending can lead to debts. But, the advantage is in the fact that you can easily identify the motivation for your expenditures and can therefore develop the tips to cut retirement costs.

The *Emotional shoppers* can buy anything at slight persuasion. Be wary of this category but rather, channel your emotions into well-researched investment-related purchases. *Debtors* may never pay or would delay the balances of earlier purchases. They spend more than they earn.

Savers will save even the last unit of the currency. They are the greatest believers in the proverbial 'rainy day' adage. They avoid debts and accumulate as much as their capacity can take them. They normally miss out of enjoying themselves.

Bargain hunters negotiate and are more interested in the final purchase price than in the value of the product. Are you a bargain hunter? It is advisable you give thoughts to the value of any investment opportunity rather than being rushed into a bargain. For instance, understanding the fact that the seller is the ultimate beneficiary in a discount or promotion price is important. This is because the buyer will certainly spend money he/she would ordinarily not spend in such situation.

Sharers often fault themselves when they do not share with others. They would share even for the fun of it. Can you continue with this habit in retirement? And, the *Risk takers* would always exploit opportunities for higher returns. In as much as it is advisable to take calculated risks, it is dangerous to be involved in risky investments. Are you of the risk taker category? Always watch out for the fundamentals, the investment cycle, the economics and the general business climate. Whichever personality category you belong, remember that 'hunger, cold, hard work, contempt, suspicion, unjust approach are disagreeable; but debt is infinitely worse than all'.

Certainly, you must create immediate and long term budgets, consciously cut down or totally eliminate unnecessary expenditures, harmonise your financial plan with your spouse, protect yourself from scams as they may even originate from family members and seek professional assistance in attempts at increasing your financial investments. It is not advisable to use gratuity for non-interest generating investments. There is a common financial counsel that you 'live below your means; diversify your portfolio and be patient'.

3. Socials

You must declare a retirement manifesto; what do I want in retirement? Imagine and create your future, connecting the past, present with the future. Be willing to try on something new and play the game full-out. How creative or original is your manifesto? Does it truly reflect you and your environment? Does it give back to your community? Remember the words of Mother Theresa 'it is not how much we give but how much love we put in the giving'.

Association with people is important. People who place more importance on relationships tend to be happier and more fulfilled life. One very important assignment in retirement is creating and maintaining friendships. Friendship is needed in retirement. Friendship boosts energy, refreshes perspectives and can excite mentorship among the younger folks. In the words of Jane Gill-Wilson 'friends are the sunshine of life'. It may not be in the number of acquaintances you encounter on a day-to day basis but in the closeness you may have with a few. Friendship begins with the family. Describing a friend, Mark Twain says 'the true office of a friend is to side with you when you are in the wrong. Nearly anybody will side with you when you are in the right'. You may learn from friends but, do not look to them for direction or approval.

Achievers in every field of endeavour are always guided by their own lights. Therefore, your self esteem is important in your relationships. Man is a reflection of thoughts stored in his unconscious. The unconscious cannot discriminate between truth and falsehood. A negative self-esteem consistent with hostility, prejudice, apathy, indecision and ignorance will not do you any good. But a positive self esteem of sympathy, acceptance, interest, responsibility and knowledge attributes will define your true relationship with people. Your relationships and associations should be based on a positive self-esteem. On the other hand, loneliness is dangerous. Researchers at the University of Chicago opined that loneliness is likely to increase the chance of death by 14%.

You may travel as many times as you can. Travel helps in exploration and in making new discoveries. Travelling can bring new experience. It may not necessarily be in terms of the long distance, but a change of environment, an adventure and fun. The longer you remain in a particular place the higher the chances of getting disillusioned with the environment. According to Miriam Beard '... travel is more than the seeing of sights; it is a change that goes on, deep and permanent, in the ideas of living'. Deacon Sylvester Ekong, a 78 years retired nurse gets 'more energy and refreshed' each time he is driven around the streets of Uyo, an activity he does twice in a month. You may also learn a new skill or play new instruments.

As I conclude I will not fail to mention the invisible hand of creation in retirement matters. It may affect you and change your story. Two stories will amplify my thoughts in this. On a certain date in July 2005, Sir Michael Udofia (*KJW*) a retired Permanent Secretary in the Akwa Ibom Civil Service of Nigeria, got a telephone call from his State governor informing him to get prepared for his (Udofia's) inauguration as a Deputy Governor. The occupant of the office had just resigned his appointment. Issues that triggered the resignation had nothing to do with Sir Udofia who was serving his community (in retirement) in a less visible role. Surprisingly, he ended in the position of a Deputy State Governor (July 2005 – May 2007) which has a mouth-watering pension arrangement for life.

In 2019, Femi Ade (not real name) retired from a Foreign Service career and hoped to settle at home. He utilised substantial part of his savings and pension into building a state of the arts events centre. This was his retirement settlement plan with a promise. With the building completed, he paid for the furniture which was to be delivered in March 2020 for the inauguration sometime in April 2020. This was not to be. The period coincided with the appearance of Covid-19 disease which put the expected business in a very bleak situation.

What played out from the two stories is that both had prepared. One may have been termed lucky and the other, unlucky. The fact is the invisible hand that can appear in our circumstances just like it did on the two. But, we must always have our plans for retirement. Circumstances should only modify such plans.

And in all these, remember your maker and expect to meet with him at any time He beacons, so make plans for your estate just as you plan to meet with Him. As I congratulate you on your meaningful retirement life, I want to leave you with the words of Oscar Wilde, 'a man who is master of himself can end a sorrow as he can invent a pleasure. I don't want to be at the mercy of my emotions. I want to use them, to enjoy them, and to dominate them'. I urge you to dominate your emotions as you enjoy a retirement life of purpose.

REFERENCES

1. Goss, S. C. (2010). The Future Financial Status of the Social Security Program. *Social Security Bulletin* Vol. 70, No3.
2. American's Perspectives on New Retirement Realities and Longevity Bonus: A 2013 Merrill Lynch Retirement Study, conducted in Partnership with Air Wave Retrieved on March 4, 2018 from https://agewave.com/wp-content/uploads/2016/07/2013-ML-AW-Americans-Perspectives-on-New-Retirement-Realities-and-the-Longevity-Bonus.pdf
3. MIT AgeLab Research Retrieved on March 29, 2020 from https://www.hartfordfunds.com/investor-insight/mit.html
4. Organisation for Economic Cooperation and development: Financial Education and Saving for Retirement. Retrieved on March 28, 2020 from http://www.oecd.org/finance/private-pensions/39197801.pdf
5. 6RetireesSharetheirSecondCareerStoriesRetrievedonJune10,2020fromhttps://www.alwaysbestcare.com/6-retirees-share-their-second-career-stories/
6. Frederick H and Kuratko, D.F. (2013). Entrepreneurship: Theory, Process and Practice. South Melbourne: Cengage Learning Australia
7. Three Consultants Success Stories By Jeff Yang. Retrieved on June 10,2020 from https://www.cbsnews.com/news/three-consultant-success-stories/
8. This 105 Year Old Martini…Moves. Retrieved on June 10, 2020 from https://steemit.com/longevity/@finprep/this-105-year-old-martini-lover-has-been-retired-for-almost-40-years-here-are-her-smartest-money-moves
9. Stumbling Towards Retirement By Peter Bloom. Retrieved on June 10, 2020 from https://www.linkedin.com/pulse/stumbling-towards-retirement-peter-bloom/
10. http://www.bbc.co.uk/newsbeat/article/38689565/what-american-presidents-do-when-they-leave-the-white-house. Retrieved on November 12, 2020
11. Huixin Bi and Sarah Zubairy, 2019. Public Pension Reforms and Fiscal Foresight: Narrative Evidence and Aggregate Implications Retrieved from https://www.hec.ca/en/iea/seminars/20191204_Sarah_Zubairy.pdf on 11/22/2020.

APPENDIX

Some Frequently Asked Questions on the Implementation Of The Contributory Pension Scheme (CPS)
Source: https://www.pencom.gov.ng/wp-content/uploads/2018/04/FAQ-CPS-reviewed.-17-Apr.-2018.pdf

1) **When Does the Deduction of Pension Contributions of a New Employee Commence?** An employer is obliged to commence the deduction of pension contributions for a new employee from his first salary.
2) **What Comprises an Employee's Monthly Emoluments?** The PRA 2014 defines 'monthly emoluments" as total monthly basic salary, housing allowance and transport allowance.
3) **What is Annual Total Emolument (ATE)?** An employee's Annual Total Emolument is the total sum of basic salary and allowances payable as his/her remuneration for one year, as may be provided under the salary structure or terms and conditions of his/her employment.
4) **How Does the Federal Government Remits the Pension Contributions of its Employees into their RSAs?** The Pension contributions of FG or employees of Treasury Funded Ministries, Departments and Agencies (MDAs) are deducted at source and lodged into a Contributory Pension Account with the CBN. The Commission computes the pension contributions and advises the CBN to credit the contributions directly to the PFCs. However, for Federal Government employees who are already on the Integrated

Payroll and Personnel Information System (IPPIS), the Office of the Accountant General of the Federation (OAGF) remits their contribution to their respective PFCs.

5) **How Does Movement from One Employment to Another Affect Pension Contribution?** Movement from one employment to another does not affect pension under the CPS. Upon change in employment, the employee is only required to give the new employer his/her existing RSA details into which payment of subsequent monthly pension contributions would continue.

6) **What Happens to the Accrued Pension Benefits of Employees Who Were Hitherto in the Services of States and Local Governments, but Later Transferred Their Services to the Federal Government After the Commencement of the CPS?** The PRA 2014 has, for the purposes of payment of retirement benefits in the public service of the Federation and FCT, abolished the practice of "transfer of service". Consequently, employees who transferred their services after the enactment of the PRA 2004 have the responsibility to arrange with their previous employers to pay their retirement benefits for the periods they worked for the previous employers.

7) **What Happens to an Employee of a Treasury-Funded MDA whose Pension Contribution is not Being Remitted to the RSA?** Such an employee should write a complaint to his PFA. He may also inform the Pension Desk Officer (PDO) and provide all necessary documents, as maybe advised by the PFA, for onward delivery to the Commission. The documents will be verified and the necessary remittance of his/her accumulated contributions would be made in all verified cases.

8) **Can an Employee Make Voluntary Contribution into His/ Her RSA?** The PRA 2014 allows employees to, in addition to the 18% employee and employer contributions, make voluntary contributions into their RSAs.
9) **Can a Person Who is Already Receiving Pension Under the Old Scheme, Make Contributions Under the New Scheme Upon Securing New Employment?** Subject to such guidelines as may be issued from time to time by the Commission, an existing pensioner may make voluntary contributions under the scheme.
10) **Are Voluntary Contributions Made by Employees Subject to Tax Deductions?** The PRA 2014 stipulates that pension contributions made by an employee under the Scheme shall not be taxed. However, income earned on voluntary contribution would be taxed if withdrawn before 5 years from the date the contribution was made.
11) **What Happens When an Employer Fails to Remit its Employees' Pension Contributions Within 7 Working Days After the Payment of Salaries?** Such employer shall in addition to making the remittance already due, be liable to a penalty to be stipulated by the Commission, which will be paid to the employees, provided that the penalty shall not be less than 2% of the total contribution that remains unpaid for each month while the default continues.
12) **Can an Employer or a Union Influence its Workers or Members to Choose a Particular PFA?** The choice of a PFA for the purpose of opening an RSA is the exclusive preserve of an employee. Neither the employer nor a Labour Union is allowed to influence employees' choices of PFAs. It is,

therefore, illegal for any employer or Labour Union to impose a particular PFA on its employees or members.

Some Frequently Asked Questions On Payment Of Retirement Benefits Under The Contributory Pension Scheme (CPS)

1. **What is the Minimum Period Required by an Employee to Qualify for Pension Under the New Scheme?** There is no qualifying period for pension. If an employee works for an employer, his pension contribution will be paid by the employer into the employee's RSA for the period of his service. However, access to the contributions must be in line with the provisions of the PRA 2014.
2. **Will Gratuity be Paid Under the CPS?** Upon retirement, an employee can withdraw a lump sum from the balance standing to the credit of his/her RSA provided the balance after the withdrawal could provide an annuity or fund monthly payments through programmed withdrawals. However, an employer may choose to pay any other severance benefits (by whatever name called) over and above the retirement benefits payable to the employee under the PRA 2014.
3. **What is Retirement Bond?** The Retirement Bond represents the accrued retirement benefits for the past services rendered by employees of the Treasury Funded Ministries, Departments and Agencies of the FGN, State and Local Governments before the commencement of the CPS. The amount is calculated by qualified actuaries and is transferred to the RSA upon retirement.
4. **Are Pension Benefits for Services Rendered Under Old Scheme Going to be Paid to the Contributors Under the CPS?** Every employee is entitled to pension and gratuity that may have accrued under the old pension scheme. The

total accrued benefit is calculated and provisions made by employers to credit the amounts determined to the respective RSAs of the beneficiaries.

5. **What are the Components of the Final RSA Balance of a Treasury-Funded FGN Employee?** The RSA balances are made up of two components, namely, accrued rights and accumulated monthly pension contributions including the investment income. The accrued rights include gratuity and pension that an employee is entitled to for the past services rendered to the FGN, from the date of his/her first appointment to 30 June, 2004.
6. **What is the Retirement Age Under the Pension Reform Act 2014?** The Act did not stipulate any retirement age. Retirement age depends on each employee's terms and conditions of employment.
7. **What Happens When an Employee Who Has Been Contributing Under CPS Dies Before His Retirement?** Where an employee who has been contributing under the CPS dies before his/her retirement, his benefits shall be paid to his beneficiary as he/she provided under a will or to the next of-kin. In the absence of such designation, the benefit shall be paid to any person appointed by the Probate Registry as the administrator of the estate of the deceased.
8. **What Happens to an Employee Who Retired Under the CPS Due to Physical or Mental Incapacity, but Subsequently Had His Case Reviewed and Recertified Fit and Proper for Employment?** Such an employee may re-enter the Scheme upon securing a new employment. The new employer would commence remittance of the employee's pension contributions into his original RSA.

9. **What Happens When an FGN Employee Receives Promotion After Enrolment Exercise?** Where a FGN employee is promoted after enrolling for the payment of accrued pension rights with the Commission, a copy of the promotion letter indicating grade level and step and effective date should be forwarded to the Commission along with a copy of his/her registration slip obtained during the enrolment exercise. These will be used to compute and pay any difference in the accrued benefits that may occur as a result of the promotion.
10. **What Do I Do if I was Unavailable and Missed the Annual Enrollment Exercise?** Any FGN employee who misses the annual enrolment can come to the Commission for the in-house enrollment, which normally commences two (2) months after the conclusion of the annual enrollment and ends two (2) months before the next annual exercise.
11. **When Can I Have Access to the Money in My RSA?** A holder of an RSA shall have access to his/her RSA upon retirement based on condition of service or upon attaining the age of 50 years (whichever is later) or is medically incapacitated. Where an employee voluntarily retirees, disengages or is disengaged, he/she can have access to 25% of his/her RSA provided that such employee is unable to secure another employment after 4 (four) months of such retirement.
12. **What Happens to the Balance in the RSA After Any Initial Lump Sum Withdrawal?** The balance in the RSA will be applied towards the payment of monthly pension to the retiree on programmed withdrawal. In the case of annuity, it is applied to procure a monthly annuity for life from a Life Insurance company.

13. **Can I Make a Lump Sum Withdrawal of More than 25% of My RSA Balance at Retirement?** This can be allowed provided the amount left in the RSA after that lump-sum withdrawal shall be sufficient to fund a Programmed Withdrawal or annuity of not less than 50% of the retiree's annual remuneration as at the date of retirement.
14. **What is Programmed Withdrawal?** This is a mode of withdrawal by which a retiree receives pension through his Pension Fund Administrator (PFA) on a monthly or quarterly basis over an estimated life-span. The RSA balance is being re-invested by the PFA to generate more income/funds for the retiree. When a retiree dies, any balance in the RSA will be paid to the duly nominated beneficiaries.
15. **What is Annuity?** Annuity is a stream of income purchased from a Life Insurance company. It provides a guaranteed periodic income (pension) to a retiree throughout his/her life after retirement. Under the CPS, annuity is guaranteed for ten years. If the retiree dies within ten years of retirement, the monthly annuity/pension will be paid to his beneficiaries for the remaining years up to ten years. For example, if a retiree who chose annuity dies six years after retirement, his monthly annuity/pension will be paid to his beneficiaries for the next four years. The retiree can buy annuity contract by paying a portion of his retirement benefits as premium to an insurance company which in turn provides the monthly/quarterly payments (annuity), subject to the Regulations jointly issued by the National Pension Commission and National Insurance Commission.
16. **What Happens to a Retiree with an Insufficient Balance in his RSA?** A retiree who has contributed for a specified

number of years shall be entitled to a guaranteed minimum pension, which will be determined by the Commission from time to time, under the Guidelines for Minimum Pension Guarantee (MPG).

17. **How Would a Person Who Retires Before the Age of 50 Years and in Accordance with the Terms and Conditions of His Employment Access his RSA?** As stipulated in Section 7(2) of the PRA 2014, this category of employees is entitled to withdraw not more than 25% of their RSA balances as at the time of retirement provided they have been out of job for 4 months and have not secured another employment.
18. **What are the Reasons for Monthly Pension and Lumpsum to Differ Between Colleagues Who Retired at the Same Time and on the Same Salary Grade?** Monthly pension and lumpsum may differ due to the following reasons: their grades, ranks, salary steps may differ as at June 2004; the magnitude of their contributions to RSA may vary during their pension accumulation phases; their respective PFAs may operate different strategies for investment of pension fund and generate different investment incomes; and they may at retirement, withdraw different amounts as lumpsum giving higher monthly pension to the one who withdrew lower amount as lumpsum due to higher RSA balance after the lumpsum withdrawal.
19. **What Constitutes the Consolidated Benefits of a Deceased Employee Who Died in Active Service?** The consolidated benefits of a deceased employee include the proceeds of his/her accumulated contribution plus any income that accrued from investing the contributions, benefits from life insurance policy and accrued pension benefits.

20. **What is the Procedure for Accessing the RSA of a Deceased Employee?** Upon the death of an employee, the employer/ Next of Kin (NoK) or representative of the deceased shall notify the PFA, who in turn shall inform the Commission with supporting documents. The deceased's consolidated benefits are, thereafter, paid in bulk to the Executors of his estate or to any person appointed by the Probate Registry as the Administrator of his estate to enable them apply the same in favour of his beneficiaries. The employer should also process the proceeds of the life insurance policy and ensure payment by the insurance company to the beneficiary.
21. **How Would the Consolidated Benefits of an Employee Who Died Prior to Opening an RSA be Processed in Favour of His Beneficiaries?** For a deceased person who did not open a RSA before his death, the NoK should open a Death Benefit Account (DBA) with any PFA of his/her choice through which the deceased's entitlements and proceeds of Life Insurance Policy would be paid.
22. **What Happens to the Benefits of a Missing Employee?** Section 9 of the PRA 2014 stipulates that where a missing employee is not found within a period of one year from the date he was declared missing and a Board of Inquiry set up by the Commission concludes that it is reasonable to presume that the employee is dead, the consolidated benefits of such missing employee would be paid by the PFA in bulk to the Executors or the Administrator of the Estate of the deceased person in accordance with section 8 of the PRA 2014.
23. **What is the Quantum of an Employee's Benefits Under the Life Insurance Policy?** Section 4(5) of the PRA 2014 makes it mandatory upon every employer to maintain a life

insurance policy in favour of its employees for at least 3 times the annual total emolument of the employees. The employer is still obligated to pay the equivalent amount of the Group Life insurance to the deceased beneficiaries in the event that it does not have a current Policy with an Insurance Company.

24. **Who Pays the Premium for a Group Life Insurance Policy?** The premium for Group Life Insurance Policy is to be paid by the Employer. The employee does not bear any cost to this effect.
25. **Are Employees Covered for Life in the Group Life Insurance Under PRA 2014?** No. Employees are covered for the period in which they are in active service of the employer. Hence, the policy does not cover the employee after disengagement/ retirement from the service of the employer.
26. **Who Provides the Group Life Insurance for the Employees of Treasury Funded Federal Government Employees?** The Federal Government provides Group Life Insurance cover for her employees through the coordination of the Office of the Head of Service of the Federation (OHOSF).
27. **Can an Employer Pay for More than the Three Times the Total Annual Emolument of the Employee?** Yes. The guideline issued by the Commission and NAICOM provides that any employer that has an existing policy whose terms are better than 3 times the Annual Total Emolument (ATE) should maintain such policy. Therefore, the employer may provide life insurance cover over and above the minimum required.
28. **Can I Choose Programmed Withdrawal and Later Change to Annuity When I Have Already Retired?** Yes. It is possible for a retiree to change to Life Annuity after collecting his

retirement benefits through Programmed Withdrawal for some time. At that time, the remaining balance in the RSA will be utilized as premium to purchase the Life Annuity from an insurance company, which will be paying him monthly pension/annuity for life.

29. **Can I Choose Annuity and Later Change to Programmed Withdrawal When I Have Already Retired?** At the moment this is not allowed. Once a retiree has chosen to collect his benefits by annuity, he is not allowed to change back to Programmed Withdrawal. The retiree can only change his annuity contract from one insurance company to another after two years based on the Surrender Value between the insurance companies. 30. How Long Does it take to Obtain Approval for Payment of Benefits? The timeline for approval of benefits payment is not more than five (5) working days from the date the Commission receives the application and supporting documents from the PFA. 31. Can Pensioners Under the Contributory Pension Scheme Benefit from Any Subsequent Increase in Salary of Workers? The PRA 2014 provides that pension should be increased after every five years or whenever there is increase in the salaries of active workers in line with the provisions of Section 173 of the 1999 Constitution (as Amended).